To Westport-South Beach Historical Society members who have helped bring the past to the present.

McCausland, Ruth L.
July 25, 1919

WASHINGTON'S

WESTPORT

by

RUTH McCAUSLAND

Drawings by BOB McCAUSLAND

THE
DONNING COMPANY
PUBLISHERS

The Donning Company/Publishers
184 Business Park Drive Suite 106
Virginia Beach, VA 23462

Second printing, 2013

Gorham Printing
3718 Mahoney Drive
Centralia, WA 98531

Library of Congress Cataloging-in-Publication Data:

McCausland, Ruth, 1919–

Washington's Westport / by Ruth McCausland : illustrations, Robert D. McCausland.

p. cm.

Includes bibliographical references and index

ISBN 1–57864–033–4 (alk. paper)

1. Westport (Wash.)—History. 2. Westport (Wash.)—Pictorial works. 3. Westport (Wash.)—Economic conditions. 4. Business enterprises—Washington (State)—Westport. I. Title.

F899.W47M33 1998

979.7'95—dc21

98–4381

CIP

Printed in the United States of America

Contents

Preface

There are at least twelve cities and towns in the United States that go by the name "Westport," as well as several in the Canadian provinces, in Ireland, and in New Zealand. For the past few years, representatives of the *Westports of the World*, a loosely-formed organization, have been meeting annually at whichever town has had the honor of being a host. Westport in Washington State was a host in 1990 and is looking forward to doing so again in 1998. Many persons, whether visiting or living here, have wondered about the origins of Washington's Westport. It is hoped this book will give some answers as to how it came into being.

What we know today about the discovery of the Grays Harbor area and its early history is found in the diaries, journals and logs kept by the first people who came here, copies of which can be found in our local library system. As few or no photographs were taken of the early days, artist Bob McCausland, after reading these accounts and being familiar with the environment, has used his imagination when doing the illustrations.

Many longtime residents, city employees and business people were most cooperative in sharing their remembrances and memorabilia. This work would never have been published without the encouragement of Dorothy Adkins, President of Westport-South Beach Historical Society, who, along with Les Morgan, helped in the selection and development of the photographs which were taken from the Historical Society collection unless otherwise noted.

Greatly appreciated also is the assistance of Suzanne Parks, the computer contributions of Dorothy Warford, and in particular the hours of time unconditionally given by Barbara Aue with her editing, refining and professional expertise when preparing the manuscript. To all the above, a sincere thank you.

Ruth L. McCausland

Introduction

It is believed the first human beings who settled along the northern Pacific Ocean coast of the United States crossed the land bridge from Asia, temporarily formed centuries ago during the Ice Age. This may or may not be true, as the people had no written language but passed their history verbally from generation to generation. They often created myths along the way to suit their interpretation of events which could not be explained within their realm of knowledge.

Over time, small groups became tribes which took possession of territories. They often lived inland along the banks of rivers during the winter months, and in the summer they would come out to the coast to set up camps where they harvested seasonal foods. They roamed across the sparsely-settled land, encountering people only of their own race. Bodies of water were their highways and canoes their main method of transportation. They traded food with other tribes and just as often warred with them. They took slaves from each other, too, the numbers of which signified a measure of one's wealth.

After the discovery that wind could propel vessels by using sails, people in other lands built ships capable of long-distance ocean travel, allowing adventurers to go forth into the unknown.

Some of the ships disappeared into stormy seas. Many more were lost when approaching land as boats with sails were at the mercy of wind and tide and had little control when maneuvering around coastal sand bars or jutting rocks. Seamen learned to carry or tow small boats for use in exploring the coastline while the larger ships were anchored offshore, sometimes several miles out.

Travels of these first explorers are well documented. In the 1500s, the Spaniards reached and conquered Mexico, establishing posts from which their ships sailed the Pacific Ocean waters. One of their pilots, a Greek whose Spanish name was Juan de Fuca, had sailed northward from Mexico. In 1593 he found the entrance to a body of water which he claimed was the Strait of Anion, the elusive Northwest Passage which was thought to connect the Pacific Ocean with the Atlantic Ocean by crossing the continent. Though the Strait bears his name, de Fuca did not venture far eastward and never knew the open water would soon be locked in by land.

Vitus Bering, a Dane in the employ of the Russian government, came from the Orient in the early 1700s and opened the way for Alexander Baranof to discover the abundance of sea otters in the Aleutian Islands. Furs became the impetus that brought white men to this remote corner of the globe.

Hudson's Bay Company, based in London, established posts in Canada, hiring English and French voyageurs to trap and trade furs. These men, hunting small land animals, moved steadily westward until they too, reached the Pacific coast. In the late 1700s, English explorers sailed the long and hazardous journey around the tip of South America and followed the Pacific coastline to reach the Northwest. The Americans from the new country of the United States followed that route.

These are a few of the events that led to the settlement of the Pacific Northwest and, in particular, the town in Washington State which goes by the name of Westport. The land on which it is located has had several names. For simplification reasons, the sand spit on the south entrance to Grays Harbor will be referred to as "Chehalis Point" up to the year 1891 when the town was officially designated as "Westport."

PART I

A New Land To Conquer

Early Area Exploration

In the 1770s when sailing ships were exploring the edges of the seas with increasing confidence, British Captain James Cook made several voyages, one of which brought him to the northwestern corner of the American Continent. When he returned to England, Captain Cook brought news that a lucrative fur market was being overlooked by British merchants. This report traveled to Boston, Massachusetts, through Charles Bulfinch, an American architectural student in London, who returned to his home in 1787. As a result, his father and five other businessmen formed a syndicate to test the market.

The group bought two ships and hired two captains, John Kendrick to command the *Columbia Rediviva* and Robert Gray to command the *Lady Washington*. The first trip began on October 1, 1787, when the two ships left Boston for a journey which was to take almost a year. They had many harrowing experiences, lost each other enroute, but they finally reached Nootka Sound on the coast of Canada. Other fur buyers were there, including Captain John Meares, a Britisher who had recently discovered the entrance to Shoalwater (Willapa) Bay, though his ship, *Felice Adventurer*, did not cross the Willapa bar into the harbor.

For some reason, at the instigation of Captain Kendrick, the captains of the two ships exchanged commands. Captain Gray, now aboard the *Columbia*, delivered a shipload of furs to a buyer in Canton, China. He picked up a cargo of tea, sailed westward

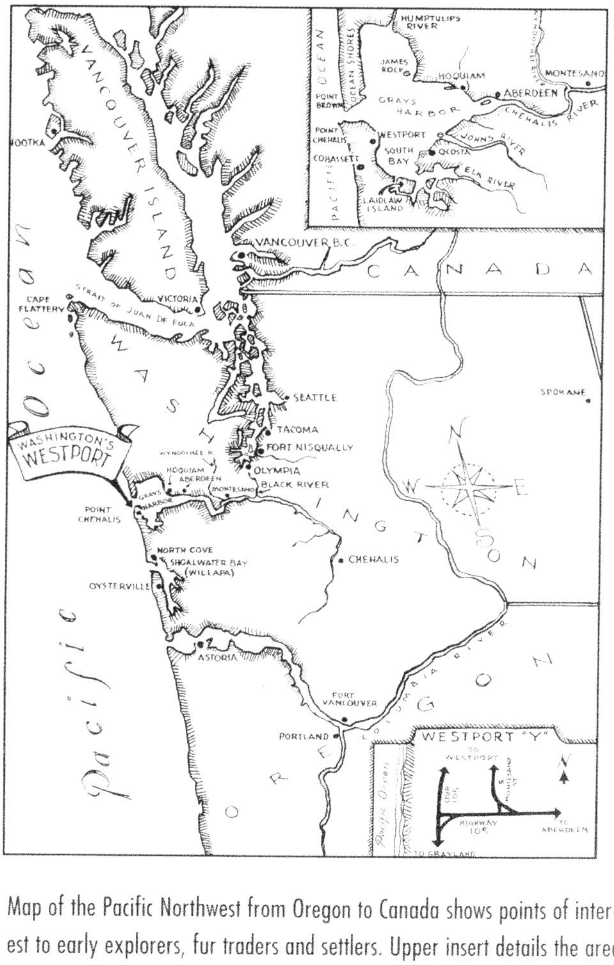

Map of the Pacific Northwest from Oregon to Canada shows points of interest to early explorers, fur traders and settlers. Upper insert details the area around Grays Harbor. Lower insert is of the "Y"; north roads lead to Westport, south road parallels the Pacific Ocean beach to Willapa Harbor. The area is known as South Beach.

around the Cape of Good Hope, crossed the Atlantic Ocean to Boston, and became the first commander of an American ship to circumnavigate the globe.

Grays Harbor Named

Although the venture was not a success monetarily, the syndicate decided to send the *Columbia* back to the Northwest. Captain Gray left Boston in 1790 and arrived at Nootka Sound the following year. He again collected furs for an oversupplied market, then decided early in 1792 to sail down the coast to look for the mouth of a great river he thought he had seen four years earlier. When he came to the head of the Strait of Juan de Fuca, he saw the *H.M.S. Discovery* commanded by Captain George Vancouver, who was on an exploration mission for the British Royal Navy. The officers of the two ships exchanged news. Captain Gray informed the Englishman of a river he had discovered, the bar of which he was unable to cross at the time. Several days later, the *Columbia* again set sail southward. On May 7th, Captain Gray saw signs of what he thought was the river flowing out between two jutting pieces of sandy beach and dropped anchor outside its entrance.

Though sea otters are near extinction due to over harvesting, there remain some of the seals which escaped the fur traders and which are rebuilding their numbers in the North Pacific islands. Thor Lauritzen photo.

With the jolly boat leading the way, the *Columbia* was able to find a deep enough channel through the sand bars, allowing the ship to arrive safely on the north side of a large bay. Once anchored, the ship was surrounded by canoes carrying well-armed Indians.

At first the Americans assumed they were the first white men the Indians had seen. They soon realized there had been previous encounters with traders, as the following day, the canoes came back loaded with beaver and otter skins. The Indians were ready to trade for blankets and iron.

Captain Gray named the new-found harbor "Bulfinch" in honor of one of the syndicate backers in Boston. Four days later, the *Columbia* sailed out of the Harbor leaving no record of any of its crew having stepped ashore while there. On May 11, Captain Gray found the entrance to a large river which he named for his ship. Most of Captain Gray's logs from the *Columbia* were lost but, fortunately for historians, sixteen-year-old Fifth Officer John Boit had kept a complete, though sometimes inaccurate, record of the voyage.

Replica of the *Lady Washington,* a frequent visitor to Westport, built in Aberdeen, Grays Harbor, was launched in 1989 and is open for tours two hundred years after Captain Robert Gray sailed from Boston on a year's trip to Nootka Sound. *The Daily World* Photo.

When Captain Vancouver completed his mapping of Puget Sound, he, too, sailed from the Strait of Juan de Fuca, turned south and stopped at the entrance to "Gray's Harbor," as he called it. He sent Lt. Joseph Whidbey, commander of his supply ship, *Daedalus,* to explore its inland shores. Lt. Whidbey charted the north side of the entrance as Point Brown and the south side as Point Hanson, named for James Hanson, an officer with the expedition. After three days of fighting currents and tides and skirting sand islands within the Harbor, Lt. Whidbey rejoined the *Discovery.* He concluded that Grays Harbor, as it was henceforth called, was of little importance, as the shoreline was inaccessible for anchorage sites. It is doubtful if any of his group set foot on Point Hanson, the future settlement of Westport on the south side of the Harbor entrance.

Hudson's Bay On Grays Harbor

After the Vancouver Expedition moved on, the Harbor was not visited again until 1824. Hudson's Bay Company, which had posts at Fort George (Astoria) on the

Columbia River and Fort Nisqually on Puget Sound, wanted a trail made between the two. An expedition led by James McMillan included a party of forty men with three heavy flat-bottomed boats filled with provisions. The group left Astoria on November 28, crossed the Columbia River, then laboriously portaged the three boats to Shoalwater (Willapa) Bay. From there, they decided to float the boats, Indian-style, along the shore in the surf. Men in the boats guided them by using poles while others on the beach pulled them along with ropes. Before they reached Chehalis Point, the expedition cut across the sand dune, the swamplands of what is now Twin Harbors State Park, and through forests until they reached the south bay of Grays Harbor, all the time in typical November weather conditions. From then on, aboard the boats, they were able to work their way up the Chehalis River to Black River and on to Black Lake, just south of Olympia. They then portaged four miles to Puget Sound. The trip was made in ten strenuous days.

Douglas Finds Native Plants

The following year, David Douglas, a young Scottish botanist from England, came to gather plants for the Horticultural Society of London. Hudson's Bay Company, a co-sponsor, allowed Douglas transportation on its ships and lodging at its posts. Douglas used Fort Vancouver on the Columbia River as his headquarters and walked thousands of miles throughout the northwest gathering plants and seeds to send back to London. He had planned to deliver the specimens personally via a Hudson's Bay ship, but while packing his material, he tripped and fell, piercing his knee on a rusty nail. His shipment went to England while he stayed at the Fort through the winter.

Though his knee continued to plague him, he and his Indian guide started out in the spring to cover other areas along the Pacific Coast. They sailed down the Columbia River, got into rough water and lost most of their supplies. His knee worsened, but the two continued northward until they reached Chehalis Point in October, 1825. When they made camp, the chief of the Indian village across the Harbor saw their smoke. Some of his men were sent in a canoe to the campsite and brought Douglas and his guide back to the village. After a few days of food and rest, the chief loaned them the use of his canoe, and several men took them to the mouth of the Chehalis River. Douglas continued on by foot but was finally forced to return to Fort Vancouver where he stayed until his knee healed.

Douglas' main legacy to Harbor country was his name which was given to the huge trees he called "firs," (Pseudotsuga menziesii), although they are not true firs. The seeds he collected from the cones of the trees he had so admired along the banks of the Chehalis River later resulted in Douglas firs being grown in many parts of the world.

Captain Robert Gray on the *Lady Washington* and the *Columbia* discovered Grays Harbor and the Columbia River in 1792.

David Douglas for whom the Douglas Fir (Pseudotsuga menziesii) was named, came to Grays Harbor for the Horticultural Society of London in 1826.

United States Navy Commander Charles Wilkes in 1838–1842 led an expedition of six ships from New York to Cape Horn, Antarctica, Hawaii and the Pacific Northwest and gave names to many geographic locations.

Wilkes Expedition

Another thirteen years passed before the next non-Indians came to the Harbor. U.S. Navy Commander Charles Wilkes left the State of Virginia in 1838, leading a six-ship, four-year expedition around the world. On the way, scientists gathered data in South America, the South Pacific, Antarctica and New Zealand, arriving in Hawaii in 1840. From there they came to the Pacific Northwest, traveled through the Strait of Juan de Fuca and into Puget Sound. Permission had been given to the expedition to use the Hudson's Bay post at Fort Nisqually as its headquarters. Several months were spent doing extensive charting, adding to that done by the Vancouver Expedition.

When the time came to leave Puget Sound, plans were made to sail south to the Columbia River, all except a party of ten men assigned to reverse the trip made by the McMillan Expedition of 1824. Led by Midshipman Henry Eld, Jr., the group left Fort Nisqually on July 19, 1841, their two canoes loaded with supplies to last them for twenty-one days, at which time they were to rejoin the main expedition on the Columbia River.

Eld and his party reached the Chehalis River on July 25, with almost one-third of their allotted time gone. These men, inexperienced in the ways of the Indians, had considerable trouble communicating in spite of having an interpreter along. Thinking they were to acquire a large Indian canoe, they gave up much of their clothing and blankets. When the trade failed, they were forced to continue on with inadequate transportation and many of their supplies gone.

The group finally reached Grays Harbor on July 31 but with little to show in the way of mapping. On August 6th, they moved from the northeast shore of the Harbor across to what they hoped was a better location. Again, on August 10, they moved southwest, this time to the bay side of what they called "Point Chehalis." Their supplies almost gone, they found dead fish and berries to eat, barely enough to keep them alive. By now, they were sick and weak, unable to do any work.

When Eld and his men failed to rendezvous with the rest of the expedition waiting on the Columbia River, several men were sent to find them. They were rescued alive but in poor condition and were taken to Astoria to recuperate. The entire expedition took thirty-nine days instead of twenty-one, twenty-four of which were spent on Grays Harbor. The men agreed with Lt. Whidbey's opinion that the Harbor had little practical use.

First Official Area Survey Completed

Twenty years after the Wilkes Expedition came through Grays Harbor, the first official survey was done by the United States Geodetic Survey in July 1862, when Captain Lawson on the brig *Fauntleroy* arrived from Shoalwater Bay. After much difficulty, the men found the main channel, seventeen feet at the lowest tide. Before the ship left, the men had charted the entire bay. By this time, the reputation of Grays Harbor was improving. Perhaps it did have some practical use after all.

Early Settlers

During all the explorations and claiming of land by foreign countries, little or no regard was given to the people who were already living there. The natives who had settled around Grays Harbor were largely of the Chehalis Tribe, but with their notorious habit of taking slaves, their families became mixtures of other Northwestern tribes. This practice later was to become a liability as it encouraged the spreading of the diseases introduced by newcomers from other parts of the world.

Chehalis Indians Here First

The Chehalis Tribal lands covered a large territory which extended roughly from Copalis Rock, about ten miles north of Point Brown, south to a point halfway between Grays Harbor and Willapa Bay, east to what is now known as Centralia and on into the southeastern Chehalis River Valley. The Indians used other fishing camps and small settlements during parts of the year, but their main village was on Chehalis Point. At one time, the village was populated by five thousand individuals. The people built their houses in the sand dunes by digging hollows three to four feet deep, walled them with two-inch thick cedar planks four to five feet high, then fastened them to a frame at the top. Roofs consisted of long planks laid lengthwise and overlapping, the peak being loose enough to open for letting the light in and smoke out. The entrance was a cedar slab which swung on a leather thong and was just large enough to cover the opening.

An Indian canoe, one of many sizes used by the Indians as they moved about Grays Harbor.

Fish was the main diet of the Chehalis, with several species of salmon available all year. Sturgeon, bottom fish, crab and razor clams were also used. This seafood was often dried or smoked over campfires, to be traded for other types of food with tribes from inland locations. Waterfowl of many kinds were supplemented with native berries during their season. Elk and deer added meat to their diet. The Indians found uses for many plants that grew locally, not only for food but for medicine, baskets and utensils.

In the summer, the men wore no clothing, the women had skirts made of grass or shredded cedar bark. They wove waterproof hats and capes from reeds, bark and roots. Later, when the white men came, the Indians traded their fish and furs for the prized wool blankets brought by Hudson's Bay Company. The blankets were draped about their shoulders and held together at the neck by a large wooden pin.

While many of the Indians traveled about to trade, to fish or to plunder, the chief of the Chehalis people lived in the village most of the year. Carcowan (Kakahwan) was chief of the Chehalis and Shoalwater Bay people when the first settlers on the Harbor arrived. Carcowan was succeeded by the highly-respected Chenamus, who dealt kindly with his white neighbors on Chehalis Point.

Beginning in the 1770s, epidemics of diseases first brought by the Spaniards swept through the Indian tribes of the Northwest. Smallpox, malaria, tuberculosis and other illnesses took their toll. In 1853 another epidemic called the "big sick" decimated the Chehalis Tribe. The fevers of this disease were so intense that the afflicted lay in the ocean water to cool. This did not cure them as they hoped, as most died. Alcohol was also given and its subduing quality contributed to the easy seizure of land by newcomers. There were few survivors and the village with its cedar shacks was abandoned, leaving only bones to give evidence of former inhabitants. With the loss of ninety percent of the Indian population, much of their culture, their history and their heritage disappeared.

What little historical evidence remains is thanks in no small part to the efforts of James G. Swan, who lived among the Indians on Shoalwater Bay and on more than one occasion visited Chehalis Point. Swan arrived at Shoalwater Bay in November 1852 and left October 1855. His land claim was on Bone River, south of Bay Center on Shoalwater Bay.

Oregon Donation Act Brings White Settlers

Seven years after members of the Wilkes Expedition came through Grays Harbor country, Oregon Territory was formed on land lying between the California and Canadian borders. Eighteen forty-eight was also the year that William O'Leary, a twenty-seven-year-old Irishman, appeared on the Harbor and is considered to be the first white settler on its shores.

Little is known about John Hole, another early settler who, sometime around 1850, built a cabin on the flats near the river where the Markham plant of Ocean Spray is presently located. He gave his name to Johns River which flows into the southeast side of Grays Harbor.

During this time, John B. Chapman and his son stopped at Chehalis Point to look at property there. They returned to Portland and advertised in an Oregon paper of beautiful land on Chehalis Point available for settlers and investors. He had no takers and dropped plans for building a city there.

Dr. Daniel V. Quenaudon may have seen the ads as he came to the Point looking for property on which to file claims for a German settlement. For a five dollar fee, members of his Oregon Colonization Society could claim three hundred acres of land plus a house lot. After filing his claim, he and Benjamin Charles Armstrong, who was looking for a mill site, went to Portland leaving a hastily-built cabin occupied by Andrew Levitt, hired as a caretaker. Levitt had little to do while on the claim except to write a diary. He did learn some of the Chinook jargon enabling him to communicate with Chief Carcowan and the few natives in the Indian village.

Levitt had been left with meager supplies but the generous Indians kept him in food. One day Captain George Phillips on the schooner *Columbia*, sailed into the Harbor to escape a storm. While there, he looked for oysters and finding none, gave some supplies to Levitt before he left. Another boat's crew who came looking for oysters and found none also gave supplies to Levitt and left.

In January 1851 Armstrong and John W. Champ came back to the Point. They surveyed Dr. Quenaudon's town site and laid out lots. Ben Armstrong took a claim as did four other men who arrived several days later. On April 17, Levitt received word that the doctor had changed his mind and gave up the claim. When Armstrong went to his new mill site on Cedar Creek, Andrew Levitt went with him.

With potential residents showing an interest in the Grays Harbor area, Ben Armstrong got his sawmill operating in 1852, east of the Harbor near the town of Oakville. He supplied lumber for many of the first buildings, boats and scows in the Chehalis Valley.

To encourage settlement, the Oregon Donation Act of 1850 was passed. It allowed any citizen of the United States, resident of the Territory, eighteen years and older, to claim 320 acres of land for himself and 320 acres for his wife. The requirement was to live on and cultivate the officially-surveyed acreage for four consecutive years. The year 1853 brought the division of Oregon Territory, with the portion north of the Columbia River becoming the Territory of Washington.

Several years previously, optimistic men from all over the country had been caught up in gold fever with the 1848 discovery at Sutter's Mill in California. They left families behind and headed for the gold fields by whatever means they could. When dreams of riches quickly dissipated, many of the disillusioned prospectors moved northward to the new Territory. An incentive to settle there was a section added to the Donation Act which allowed a person to purchase land after two years' occupancy at $1.25 an acre. This Act was in effect only until December 1, 1855, when all claims had to be filed. After that, anyone could purchase the land on which his claim was located, provided it had been officially surveyed.

Armstrong and Luark Arrive

Patterson Fletcher Luark, born in Tennessee in 1814, had moved westward with his parents during his growing years. When the family settled in Indiana where his father taught school, Luark developed his own farm in Illinois. He married, had two children, then moved to a new location in 1840. All four were suffering from an unknown illness at which time his wife and older child died. The following year Luark married Mary Hodge and, with his son, Marcellus, lived in Illinois until 1852. He then sold his farm, disposed of personal effects, paid visits to all his relatives, and prepared to join a wagon train to Puget Sound, Oregon Territory. The Luarks left in April 1853 and by October had bought a claim in Thurston County southwest of Olympia. Luark became involved in the organization of Chehalis County in 1854, and also served in several official positions. He and friends went on an exploring trip to the coast in 1857, and on August 17 they saw the Pacific Ocean for the first time.

Patterson Luark kept a journal of his life on Chehalis Point between the years 1858 and 1868.

Speake Takes Up A Claim

Thompson Barker Speake of Portland, Oregon Territory, had heard through his friend, Glenn Peterson, also from the Portland area, of good farm land available around Grays Harbor. He was so impressed that in 1857 he sold his home and moved his wife and four children, ages seven to one, with all their belongings to Washington Territory. After a circuitous trip of several weeks, they reached the Chehalis River. They loaded everything on a "flatboat," a large raft-like structure. Once aboard, they drifted down the river to Grays Harbor, across the south channel, and carried their goods to their claim on the east side of Chehalis Point, not far inland from South Bay, near where present-day Montesano Street and Ocean Avenue meet. If he followed the custom of the day, Speake used the flatboat's lumber to build a shelter, along with driftwood found on the beach. He dug a well and planted fruit trees brought from Oregon. The summer weather was warm enough so that the shack was adequate. It was another matter when winter came, as the wind blew and rain fell much of the time.

The few Indians who survived the siege of epidemics were living in the remains of their nearby village. They did not disguise their resentment towards the white family who settled there. This was no doubt a result of a treaty meeting which had taken place two years earlier. With settlers taking over land in Washington Territory, the federal government in Washington, D.C. had attempted to solve the problem of title to land once used by the Indians. Sections of this land were to be set aside and reserved for the sole use of the Indians, the rest to be surveyed and sold to settlers.

Governor Seeks Tribal Treaties

The purpose of the meeting between the entourage headed by the first Washington Territorial Governor, Isaac Stevens, and representatives of the Quinault, Queets, Cowlitz, Chehalis and Shoalwater Bay tribes was to convince Indians to relinquish all rights and titles to land used by them. They were expected to move onto one reservation, disregarding their differences in lifestyles. The terms of the agreement were translated by an interpreter and the treaty was signed on January 25, 1856, but by only the Quinault and Queets leaders. The Senate confirmed the treaty on March 8, 1856, and President Franklin Pierce signed the paper establishing the Quinault Indian Reservation on the north side of Grays Harbor.

The Indian leaders of Chehalis Point and Shoalwater Bay had refused to sign. They, therefore, were not "treaty" Indians. They remained under the control of the United States Government but did not receive the same benefits given to those who did sign. A parcel of land on the east side of the county near Oakville was reserved for the Chehalis. The Shoalwater Bay Indians chose land near Tokeland. Time limits were set in which terms were to stay in effect with the assumption that the Indians would eventually be self-supporting by learning the ways of the white man. These stipulations have created many controversies which still continue to this day.

Petersons Stay Permanently

The Speake family had not been on their new claim long when their former neighbor in Portland, Glenn Peterson, came looking for land on which to settle. He made the initial move along with Thomas, Jeff and Charles Carter, Joe Payne and fifty head of cattle. They came from Montesano down the south side of the Chehalis River, along the beach to South Bay and swam the cattle across to Chehalis Point. Peterson then returned to Portland.

As the only white woman on Chehalis Point, Mrs. Speake felt so threatened by the Indians and disliked the weather so much, she begged her husband to move the family away. When Glenn Peterson returned the following year with his wife, Jane and three year old son, Frank, Speake had almost finished his cabin on his property. He turned his claim over to Peterson, took his family and left Chehalis Point for good. The Petersons proved to be the only settlers to stay permanently on the Point.

Luark Claim

In September 1857, Patterson Luark took up the claim which was vacated by John Hole at the mouth of Johns River and built a cabin on it. Two months later he moved one yoke of oxen, a cow, calf and a year old bull to the river claim. During this time, accompanied by several others, he made two more exploration trips around Grays Harbor. He noted in his diary on February 24, 1858, that he attended the sale of property belonging to the estate of Ben C. Armstrong, deceased, and purchased 9,000 feet of lumber. The next day he, with the help of W. B. D. Newman and several Indians, started blazing part of a trail along the Chehalis River to South Bay, returning home after twenty-five days of hard work. On April 8th he, along with Charles Byles and Newman, purchased more lumber from Ben Armstrong's mill, almost 40,000 feet, for the purpose of building houses on Johns River. While rafting from the mill, some of the lumber was lost and some reached the river to be stacked on its banks. However, by that time Byles and Newman had lost interest in putting up houses there.

By the end of June 1858, Luark had moved his family to the Johns River claim. Stock belonging to him and Reuben Redman arrived on July 2. By the tenth, the men had made a cattle lot to hold the animals.

Two days later Luark went to Chehalis Point to serve as judge for a general election and was elected by nine votes as Justice of the Peace. While there, Luark unsuccessfully sought a claim site, returned to Johns River for another week, then went back to the Point. This time he found a suitable site with a spring of fresh water two and a half miles southwest of the Point, one and a quarter miles south of Speake's original claim. The next day, July 20, Luark began cutting brush on his new site.

On July 23 Luark returned to Johns River. Three days later he took a small load of lumber across the bay. On the twenty-seventh, with the help of several men, he drove his stock from the mouth of Johns River to South Bay. The next day, at low tide and again with help, he crossed the channel with twenty-three head of cattle and eight

Grays Harbor shore at high tide, similar to that which greeted the Luark family in 1858.

horses. Luark led one horse by the bridle, taking the horses over first, then "boated two calves and towed an ox, driving the balance after." Luark took care to have oxen and horses near the water's edge so that the cattle could see them from the opposite side. The stock was all moved safely.

The following day Luark brought his family over to the peninsula into the thick timber between the Harbor and the Pacific Ocean. There the family lived in open air under a few boards of lumber, during which time "great quantities of rain fell."

Patterson Luark kept a diary during these years, as did his brother, Michael, who had also joined the wagon train when it left the Midwest in 1853. Copies of these diaries are available in the Research Section of Timberland Regional Library System. Spellings are not always accurate, some words indecipherable; nevertheless, the Luark's journals give a remarkable account of life as pioneers during the mid-1800s.

Not long after the Luarks moved into their lean-to, Dr. A. G. Henry and his daughter, Mrs. Aleck C. Smith, moved to the Point with her three small children. The following week, Jeff Carter, his wife and two children also arrived. With the Glenn Petersons, there were now four families living on the Point. Lyman Schaffer had claimed land on nearby Laidlaw Island, named for Alex Laidlaw, who had built a mill on the east side of the Elk River, across the bay from Chehalis Point.

On Friday, August 13, 1858, Luark recorded in his journal the following account:

"Today is the first day since we arrived on the Harbor that the sun rose clear & remained shining all day. We layed (sic) the foundation of a log house today 18 by 22 feet all surrounded with trees great & small. On the 8th I was at Chehalis and saw Mr. F. Hatch. He and his wife reside near the mouth of the Humptulips river, north side of Harbor.

"Saturday, 14th, today a melancholy occurrence happened on the Harbor casting a shade of gloom on our infant settlement. Mr. & Mrs. Hatch in company with Henry & Smiths surveying party consisting of three canoes in all left the mouth of the Humptulips at daybreak to run down to the north point here to take breakfast and then when the tide commenced flooding they intended to cross over to Chehalis Point. Mr. & Mrs. Hatch were in a small Chinook canoe well laden and second in advance. The formost (sic) canoe ran in and landed but for some unknown cause Mr. & Mrs. Hatch steered across for Chehalis Point with sail set, there being a brisk wind from the east and tide rushing out with great speed. They kept up their sail until all disappeared in the breakers. They was watched from Chehalis with great anxiety by all on the point and Thos. Carter Esq. forced out the Indians with a large Chinook hoping to rescue them but all of no avail. They both sank to rise no more. Some of the light articles came ashore with the flood tide and the canoe went ashore on the north side of Harbor but God ruleth the waves and therefore we must meekly submit."

On November 6, 1858, the first white child was born on Chehalis Point. In honor of the discoverer of the Harbor, he was named Robert Gray Luark.

As Justice of the Peace, Patterson Luark traveled around the county and was gone a great deal of the time. He stayed at the homes of his many friends, who, in turn, stayed with the Luark family when they visited Chehalis Point. On Sundays he attended church services wherever he happened to be. With his herd of cattle, Luark was able to supplement his income by selling butter, cheese, eggs and vegetables to residents of the Chehalis Valley. He planted four hundred fruit trees and, by November 1864, was able to pick forty bushels of apples from which to make cider to sell. He dug a ditch in 1860 in an attempt to drain his land, outcome unknown. In 1861, he and his neighbor, A. H. Fisher, staked an oyster bed in the bay, outcome also unknown.

The family lived on their claim for ten years, then moved back to the Montesano area. He mentioned in his diary in 1868 that he had dug potatoes on the place "I bought from John Luark." On November 10 he moved onto the Cascadell property.

Luark had nine children, three of whom preceded him in death. In 1866, his daughter, Lenora, married Francis Talbert, a nurseryman who emigrated from Wisconsin in 1859. Three years later, Nora succumbed to tuberculosis. For a time, Talbert carried mail between Olympia and Chehalis Point, then moved away.

Patterson and Mary Luark went to California in 1888, where they stayed the rest of their lives. Mary died in 1891, Luark remarried in 1894. His third wife died in 1899. Michael Luark, who lived in and around the Chehalis Valley, visited the Point often but never claimed it as his home. Both Patterson and Michael Luark died in 1901.

Natives React To White Intrusion

In many areas of the newly-settled Northwestern Territory, Indians who wanted all the white people destroyed held war councils with inland tribes. Chief Chenamus, who lived in the Indian village on the Point, met with Tyee John from across the bay to discuss the pending massacre. He emphatically stated that the Chehalis Indians wanted no part of this action as they were living in peace with the whites.

The Chehalis Point settlers' lives were spared, but some of the Indians watched the settlers constantly, following them about while they muttered amongst themselves.

The Indians did not fear the whites but rather thought of them as "crazy." When the settlers began to carry firearms for their own protection, they were watched still more carefully. In spite of the Indians' displeasure towards the settlers, this situation did not directly bring about the establishment of Fort Chehalis. Rather, it was the result in a roundabout way of the first steamer coming to ply the waters of Grays Harbor.

Captain Thomas Wright had purchased the sternwheeler *Enterprise* and used it for a short profitable time during the gold rush on British Columbia's Fraser River. In 1859 Captain Wright had run out of work and moved his boat and family to Grays Harbor, intending to transport freight and passengers from Chehalis Point to Montesano. Business proved slow. Wright also discovered that the navigational problems of the Harbor with it currents, tides and sand bars were much greater than expected.

The Army Comes To The Point

After a few frustrating months, one day Captain Wright tied the steamer to a tree at the mouth of the Chehalis River and headed for the Territorial Capital. In Olympia he told the Legislature that the local Indians were causing worrisome problems at Chehalis Point. Due to native uprisings in other parts of the Territory, his exaggerations were taken seriously, the consequence of which was troops being sent

Fort Chehalis was occupied in 1860–1861 during the Indian uprisings of Washington Territory.

from Fort Steilacoom on Puget Sound to protect the white settlers who filed claims around Grays Harbor.

On February 9, 1860, Company A, Fourth Infantry, led by Captain Maurice Maloney, arrived at the Satsop River, conveniently met by Captain Wright on the *Enterprise*. The little steamer sailed off to Chehalis Point with approximately sixty soldiers, four of whom had families along. Ten of the passengers were Americans and the

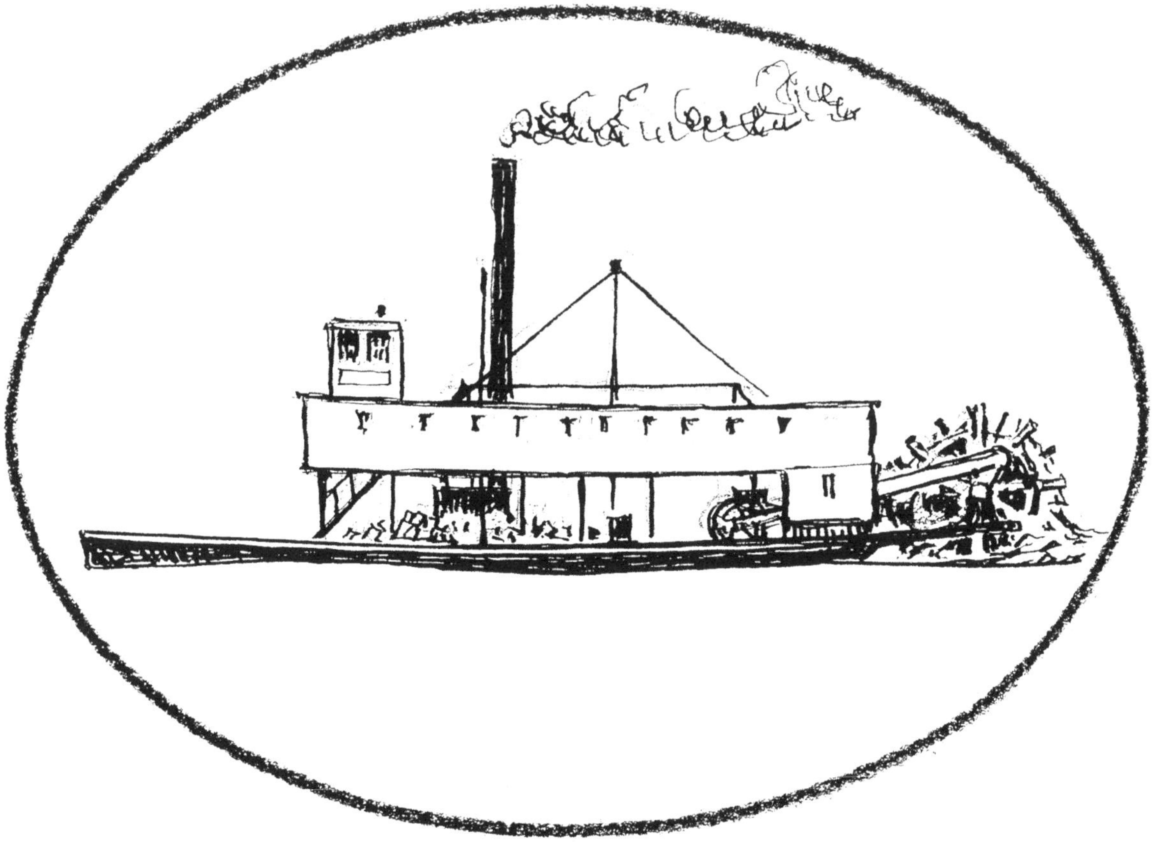

The sternwheeler *Enterprise* brought the United States Army down the Chehalis River and out to Chehalis Point in 1860.

rest Europeans. The civilian-clad soldiers were armed with muskets, bayonets and a four-foot-long field piece.

The level land site chosen for the post was part of Jay T. Carter's claim, bounded on the north by Elizabeth Street. It included sections of present-day Adams and Baker Streets, all surrounded by pine trees.

In March, the schooner *Calumet* arrived from Portland bringing supplies and freight for both the fort and the settlers. The first job was to build an 84' x 50' barracks for the men and a house for Captain and Mrs. Maloney. Sam Benn of Aberdeen assisted in the construction of five buildings, including a guardhouse made from logs. Over its short life, the military base was known as "camp," "post," and finally, "fort."

The presence of the soldiers probably did have a calming effect on the area. The biggest problem, however, was brought on by the overindulgence of alcohol by both the Indians and the whites. One day Captain Maloney felt compelled to write to the Territorial Governor about licenses granted to sell liquor in Indian country. Some merchants, including Sam Williams and Matthew McKee, were caught but not penalized. Once the land was opened to settlers, it was no longer considered Indian country. It was, however, illegal for anyone to sell liquor to Indians or to the soldiers without written permission from their commanding officer. Captain Maloney used threats to slow down that problem. Another serious situation was caused by settlers encroaching on Indian property, but at no time during their stay were the soldiers forced to protect the settlers from the Indians.

Soldiers Sent Off To War

In June 1861, two months after the outbreak of the Civil War, special orders came from Fort Vancouver requesting a prompt move from Fort Chehalis to the Columbia River where troops were to be transported on the first available steamer to San Francisco. All stores were removed and the buildings left vacant.

Within a short time, trouble was brewing on the north side of Grays Harbor where there were considerably more Indians. On July 20 the acting governor of the Territory of Washington, Henry M. McGill, sent a letter enclosing seven affidavits written by settlers to W. W. Miller, Superintendent of Indian Affairs in Olympia. He wrote, "In consequence of the withdrawal of troops from Fort Chehalis, the savages have assumed an attitude of hostility and in some cases have caused the settlers to abandon their farms. Great fears are entertained of further violence."

The letter was forwarded to Colonel Wright, Commanding Officer at Fort Vancouver who, in turn, ordered Second Lieutenant C. D. Emory, Ninth Infantry officer, to take eleven soldiers to Fort Chehalis, along with supplies to last until September 20. They were to help establish a post for the Indian agent on the Quinault Indian Reservation at Taholah, about thirty-five miles north of the Fort, hoping to quell a potential uprising. The detachment arrived at Fort Chehalis on August 15 to await the arrival of the Indian agent. Lieutenant Emory wrote to his superior that there were "about thirty Indians, men, women and children at Chehalis Point, and some fifty more in the Shoalwater Bay area, all peaceable in character."

Patterson Luark noted in his diary that on Saturday, August 17, "W. W. Miller, Superintendent of Indian Affairs, with a crew of employees for the Queniult (sic) reservation arrived at Chehalis this afternoon, J. W. Anderson from the Cowlitz being the Agent for said reserve." The next day "Indian Superintendent, troops etc., all crossed the mouth of the Harbor for Point Grenville."

Though problems were still evident across the bay, the Army recalled all their personnel to take part in the Civil War. Attempt was again made to keep a small force at Fort Chehalis but it was not to be. The Army suggested that a volunteer civilian force be formed. They apparently were not needed as no further uprisings were reported. The buildings at Fort Chehalis remained intact until after the Civil War was settled. They were then sold for scrap lumber or dismantled and rebuilt elsewhere.

With all these added activities, business increased and Captain Thomas Wright's financial difficulties were solved, temporarily. One day only a few weeks after the arrival of the troops, the *Enterprise* hit a sand bar near the entrance to Grays

Harbor and became wedged too firmly to be moved. In June 1860 the schooner *Calumet* took the machinery and as much equipment as could be salvaged from the *Enterprise*. (It was not reported who reaped the benefits of their sale.) In 1864 during an extremely high tide, the hull of the sternwheeler refloated and settled onto another shoal where it remained until it disintegrated.

Town, County & Territory

The First Local Store Seed For A Town

Samuel H. Williams made his appearance on Chehalis Point before the Fort was built. He had been living on the east side of Chehalis Valley. He married the daughter of Indian Agent Sidney Ford in 1852, moved to the Point around 1858, and, in partnership with Thomas Carter, opened a hotel-store-tavern business. He kept a stock of liquor in barrels, which he sold not only to the troops and residents but also to the Indians. This, of course, was illegal. After the soldiers left the Fort, he somehow managed to acquire the small cannon which had been a part of their arms and was left behind when the rest of the stores were sent to Astoria. Williams used the cannon as a signal. One shot meant he had received one barrel of whisky, two shots meant two barrels. When the shots echoed across the Harbor, the race was on to be first in line.

The store eventually was able to supply the demand, the cannon was forgotten and became the property of a saloon keeper in the town of Oysterville on Willapa Bay. One night the barkeep, in a misguided spirit of fun, blew up the cannon and some of the town of Oysterville with it.

Town Of Chehalis Platted

Thomas Carter was a member of a pioneer family prominent in the early days of Chehalis Valley, who seemed to move about as much as the Luarks, Speakes and others. Carter helped Luark make the initial move to the Point, then apparently stayed, as he filed a claim for government land there. In 1860 he and Sam Williams laid out part of the town of "Chehalis" with the intent of selling lots for homes. They named the streets after the women in their two families: Martha, Anna, Emma, Harriet, Margaret, Elizabeth and Mary.

Joseph W. McKee had a small store on the Point in 1860. He was somehow involved with possessing questionable arms and ammunition and also sold liquor to the Indians. By the following year he had left Grays Harbor.

Thomas James, third son of Samuel James, Sr., who settled on the north side of Grays Harbor near James Rock in 1852, filed a claim near the Luark place in October

1859. Luark built a cabin for Thomas and in the following weeks the James family often came across the bay to help him get established.

Samuel James, Sr. and his sons had built a 14' x 45' scow with thick sides in which iron clamps were fitted to hold railings. Onto the scow were loaded household goods, lumber and cattle. As it drifted down the Chehalis River, it was guided by long sweeps (oars) to the north shore of the Harbor, across from the Point, where their new house was built. The family lived there until 1864 but returned to Grand Mound after Samuel, Sr. had what was probably a stroke.

Other Early Settlers

Other early settlers included A. H. (Henry) Fisher who took up a claim in October 1859, south of the Patterson Luark farm. He stayed in the area for a few years, at least until 1865. Charles Johnson had a place for a short time near the Luarks but left, as did the family of W. K. Melville, one-time sheriff of Pierce County. Thomas Ford, son of Judge Sidney Ford, moved his family to Chehalis Point in 1868 but did not stay long.

As these families came to Chehalis Point, they also brought cattle for a steady source of milk and butter. The scows on which the stock was loaded were sometimes moved with sails, later towed by sternwheelers. Once there, the cattle roamed freely about the unlimited pasture land. However, they were never able to wander far because of nature's fences, the ever-present creeks and tide flats. The owners branded their cattle, but that did not always eliminate controversies over ownership. Sam Williams was once accused by Luark of butchering a steer Luark had purchased from E. L. Payne. After considerable friction, Sam Benn and Pete Carter arbitrated the case and agreed with Luark. The incident was apparently settled by the following year as Luark performed one of the first weddings in the county when Samuel Benn and Martha Redman were married on January 12, 1862, in the parlor of the home of Sam Williams.

Redman Starts Cattle Business

Reuben Redman had crossed the plains by wagon train in 1852. Traveling with him was his wife who died and was buried along the trail, leaving him with four children to raise. Redman settled on his timber claim, property which in later years was to become Ocosta. In 1858 Redman helped Patterson Luark move his stock over the first cattle trail, seven of the cattle belonging to Redman. He later bought fifty-six acres of land in Aberdeen and became a partner to Sam Benn in 1886.

Samuel Benn, born in Ireland in 1832, came to New York City as a child. He received his American citizenship, learned carpentry, but caught gold fever during the

California rush in 1849. Not until 1856 did the twenty-four year old Benn arrive in San Francisco where he located his cousin, George Hubbard but was far too late to reap the benefits from the gold fields. When Benn had earned enough money from his carpentry trade, he and Hubbard left California and headed north to the Fraser River gold find in Canada. When that, too, proved futile, the two young men bought a sailboat, loaded it with their belongings and found their way to Olympia. Though population there was sparse in 1859, much of the land was already taken, so they continued westward. They portaged their sailboat to the Black River, connected with the Chehalis River and floated down to Grays Harbor, where Benn was to spend the rest of his life. Though Sam Benn was the founder of the City of Aberdeen and was its first mayor, he spent much of his time on Chehalis Point fulfilling his duties as Chehalis County Sheriff.

By 1868, now with three children, the Benn family moved to the banks of the Wishkah River. Both Benn and his father-in-law, Reuben Redman, became involved in local governmental matters and did much to shape the future of Grays Harbor. Sam and his son, Ed, started a small commercial cranberry bog south of Cohasset in 1912. They imported plants from Cape Cod and by 1913 had acquired several hundred acres of bog land between Grays Harbor and Willapa Bay. They sold thirty tracts the following year, mostly to Finnish loggers. Thus began the cranberry industry on the South Beach.

Reuben Redman lived for ninety-seven years and died on his farm in 1917. Samuel Benn lived to be one hundred three years old, his life coming to an end on September, 16, 1935.

Washington Territory Formed

Oregon Territory was established by the United States Government on August 13, 1848. The following year, General Joseph Lane became its first governor but only after Abraham Lincoln declined the honor. The large territory was divided in 1853, the northern portion becoming the Territory of Washington. On March 21, 1854, a bill was passed by the Territorial Legislature which created Chehalis County. The bill stipulated that "the portion of Thurston County from the northwest corner of Pacific County, east to a point on the Chehalis River six miles above Armstrong's mill, north to the Mason County line, west to the Pacific Ocean, and south along the coast line of the ocean to Shoalwater Bay" was to be known as Chehalis County.

The bill also provided that the home of Captain D. K. Weldon near the mouth of North River at Bruceville (Bruceport) should be the county seat with Weldon appointed as County Treasurer. When it was discovered that North River and Bruceville were several miles apart, the county seat was designated as Bruceville, regardless of the fact that the little settlement was in Pacific County and inaccessible to most of Chehalis County.

There was much controversy over the accuracy of the county lines, understandably when one considered the lack of maps of a heavily-forested, thinly-populated land with limited means of transportation. In 1855 Oysterville was chosen to be the Pacific County seat, but not until an election in July 1860 at Chehalis Point was the new Chehalis County seat chosen. On that day, Chehalis Point had thirty-six voters, excluding women and Indians, but got only two of the seventy-four votes cast. The new county seat was to be at the Scammon home with David Mace as County Treasurer.

Scammon Family Settles In

Isaiah L. Scammon, a farmer from Maine, had responded to the lure of gold dust during the rush of 1849 in California. He was an unsuccessful prospector who traveled northward to the Chehalis Valley. He sent for his wife and children and in 1852 filed a donation claim for 640 acres of land at the mouth of the Wynooche River. In time the home of Isaiah and Lorinda Scammon became an important stopping place for travelers between Chehalis Point and inland areas.

The Scammons had four daughters, the last having been born after the move to Washington Territory. Another Scammon, Don, possibly a brother of Isaiah, also came to the Valley. George N. Scammon, who may have been a nephew of Isaiah, settled on Chehalis Point in 1859. The Grays Harbor Directory of 1911 lists his name as postmaster, clam cannery owner and general store proprietor at Westport.

Drawing The Line

Even though the two county seats had been established by 1860, there was still a problem of lines between Pacific and Chehalis Counties. In an attempt to settle the matter, a meeting was held at Chehalis Point in April 1861. No decision was made, as no representatives from Pacific County appeared. Two more years were to pass before final action was taken. In July 1863, Sam Williams was hired to take Governor William Pickering, Superintendent of Indian Affairs E. Y. Hale, Dr. A. G. Hervey, general surveyor, and Patterson Luark by wagon from Chehalis Point to Shoalwater Bay for a meeting with Pacific County officials. Before they left, Williams must have had a little too much to drink. When he saw a cow on the beach, he began to chase it with the horse and wagon carrying the dignitaries. The wagon overturned and unceremoniously dumped the passengers onto the sand. The officials were finally delivered to North Cove and the division of the counties agreed upon. Scammon's home remained the Chehalis County seat until 1886 when it was moved across the Wynooche River to Montesano.

On June 1, 1915, the name of Chehalis County was changed to Grays Harbor County.

Fry Family Ties

Within a year after the Patterson Luark family moved from the Point to the Montesano area, they became acquainted with John Fry, a newcomer to the Valley. Four Fry brothers, orphans from Illinois, had come west at different times during the mid-1800s. Jason, then seventeen years old, crossed the Plains in 1849 with his uncle, Olney, and a friend, Simeon Markham. Jason was so taken with "Oregon" country, he persuaded his brother, John, to move also. In 1851, accompanied by his wife, Margaret, baby son Charles and brother Amherst, he joined a wagon train and made the six-month journey to Oregon Territory. Reunited, Jason and John settled in the town of Rainier along the Columbia River and began logging. Amherst, age thirty, joined the Volunteers fighting the Yakima Indians but died from tuberculosis in 1857.

Annette Huntington and Jason Fry were married in 1858 and lived in Rainier. John worked in a sawmill and together with Jason, kept a herd of sixty-three cattle. The disastrous winter of 1861, coldest ever known in the Northwest, caused them to lose all but three cows. Discouraged by this loss, Jason left the Columbia River and obtained a position at the Quinault Indian Reservation teaching Indians farming methods. When he had settled in, Annette and their two sons followed him to Taholah. On July 18, 1867, the Fry family moved to Chehalis Point, staying there until April when they relocated in Montesano.

John Fry moved to Grays Harbor near Redman Creek across the Bay from Chehalis Point. By now well-acquainted with the Luarks, John started a water power lumber mill near Montesano. He had the help of Michael Luark and others. He also heard of the cattle brought by the first settlers to Chehalis Point, running wild. His mill had been doing so well that he purchased the Patterson Luark claim in 1871 and began the business of running cattle from his new home on the Point. His son, Charles, now a young man, signed a four-year contract to carry mail between Olympia and North Cove via Chehalis Point. To cover the route he had the occasional help from his father.

Twenty-four year old Charles Fry was married to Amanda Slover in 1875. Amanda, in a later interview with Ed Van Syckle, Editor of the *Aberdeen Daily World*, recalled that they and the Petersons were the only white families living at Chehalis Point at that time. After the closure of Fort Chehalis, all the other residents gradually moved away.

John and Charles Fry, along with Miles S. Griswold of Oysterville, formed a partnership to furnish stock for Richard Carruthers, also of Pacific County. The men began rounding up the unclaimed cattle and horses running wild on the Point. The Fry's payment was to keep a percentage of the herd for themselves.

Transition To Lumbering

By 1876, when the cattle business was no longer profitable, John Fry and his family moved to Oysterville on Shoalwater Bay. Three years later they moved to the east end of Grays Harbor between Aberdeen and Hoquiam. They settled on Fry Creek where John resumed his sawmilling. Shortly after the move, he became involved with Charles Stevens, owner of an unsuccessful grist mill. Jason Fry convinced John to help Stevens convert the plant to a sawmill, the beginning of the lumber industry at Cosmopolis. In 1881, John and Charles moved their families into new homes there. That same year, John was one of the businessmen who instigated the first shipment of lumber from Grays Harbor when the *Kate and Ann* left port with cedar loaded on its decks.

In 1886 John and Margaret Fry made a trip to the central United States to visit relatives they had not seen in thirty-five years. While there, they painted such a glowing picture of the Pacific Northwest that about sixty persons returned with them the following year. One of these was John's sister, Elmira, widow of Sam Van Syckle, who stayed in Cosmopolis to manage a boarding house for her brother.

When the Frys returned from the midwest, they brought back and planted the first evergreen blackberries in Harbor country. These vines adapted so easily to the climate that they can now be found growing rampant all over the Northwest.

Jason Fry had, at one time, filed a claim near Johns River, on property which held a nice stand of cedar trees. He returned to the claim at Markham, named after his pioneer friend, Simeon, and stayed there the rest of his life. He died in 1888 after a suspected attack of appendicitis.

Natural Elements & Unwanted Immigrants

Gold In Them Thar Dunes

Due to the fact that many of the settlers in the new Chehalis County had found their way north from the gold fields of California, one of them was bound to notice bits of shiny material in the sands at Chehalis Point. Three years after Sam Williams had unloaded his passengers on the beach, he was found to be involved in a gold-recovery operation on the Chehalis Point property of Mrs. Aleck Smith. Several men had a partnership, two of whom were named Henry, Mrs. Smith's maiden name, undoubtedly relatives.

A simplified version of the operation consisted of sand being pumped through sluice boxes, separating the heavier metal. Frank Peterson, now twelve years old, led the horse which gave the pump its power. The gold flecks recovered were so fine that little profit was gained from all the work that went into the operation. The partnership changed hands several times without creating wealth for anyone. Other attempts were made to mine the gold but the beach changed tremendously over the years. Once the jetty was in place, the entire shoreline moved westward with sand covering any gold deposited there. The last attempt was in 1915, also unprofitable, and the business venture was finally abandoned.

Unwanted Immigrants

Many of the weed-type plants which grow profusely in Harbor country were introduced by the early settlers. The James family brought foxglove seeds from England and passed them around to their friends. Himalaya and evergreen blackber-

Foxglove (Digitalis purpurea) seeds were brought from England by the James Family and were distributed among their friends. The flowers with cream-to-rose-colored blossoms now brighten the roadsides in late spring. Thor Lauritzen photo.

ries, also introduced, have little similarity to the small wild blackberry (Rubus ursinus) identified by David Douglas as a true native of the Northwest. Weeds such as dandelions and clover became nuisances as did some of the grasses planted in the area for pasture land feed.

Accidentally imported were insects living on some of the fruit trees and other vegetation brought in by the settlers. Patterson Luark tells in his journal of an infestation of an unfamiliar type of cutworm on his and Glenn Peterson's properties.

One of the worst insects to plague the newcomers was the little black flea, well-established long before the settlers' arrival. The fleas bred easily in the warm sands surrounding the Point. They made their homes in decaying wood, in driftwood and in the firewood brought into the houses for cooking and heat. The only method of control against these pests was by pouring scalding water onto the floors of houses and into any cracks in the walls where the fleas may have taken refuge.

PART II

When the Wind Blows

Wild Weather

As a rule, the weather along the Pacific coast stays mild much of the year. Rain brings various degrees of moisture during all seasons and is interspersed with occasional periods of drought. A cold spell in the winter causing several days of ice and snow often quickly changes back to rain. While some winters have no snowfall, or others mere dustings, there are always extremes along the Pacific coastline.

The January 1950 snowfall was unusual for Westport.

The winter of 1861 was one of those, not only on Chehalis Point but all over the Pacific Northwest. It was so cold that the Columbia River froze solid enough for heavy wagons to cross over from Washington to Oregon. A snow storm also brought a white Christmas to the settlers on Chehalis Point. Nineteen inches fell during the next weeks and traces of snow were evident until April. Four years later, in March, there were twelve inches of snow on the ground with half that depth in places inside the Luark home.

When the snow melts, floods often take over.

Over a period of many years, the ocean beach had formed a ledge topped with driftwood up to one hundred feet wide. As people moved into the area, they began to use this wood not only for home fires but also for building materials, thus reducing the barrier against high tides. Heavy winds then caused sand to cover the prairie edging along the shoreline which, in time, changed the shape of the land. This was evident on December 20, 1866 when the highest known tides caused creeks of the Point to flood the Luark's cabin, forcing the family to flee to higher ground.

Another cold winter, in 1868, caused the Chehalis River to freeze over, the only time it was known to have done so. Halfway into the next century the cold weather again made history. In January 1959, winds over seventy miles per hour struck the coast, dropping the temperature to eighteen degrees. Boats of the Westport fishing fleet were pushed into the docks to which they were moored. Water tossed about by fierce winds, froze wherever it happened to land. The weight of the boats was increased dramatically from the ice that lay thick on exposed exteriors. Snowdrifts covered the ground all around the Harbor, closing schools and businesses. Power outages added to the discomfort of the residents. By the end of the week, warm air moved in, rain fell, snow melted, and flooding changed the frozen ground into seas of mud.

People who make their homes in this area adapt to weather conditions. Precipitation amounts range from highs of over a hundred inches in a year to lows of less than fifty inches. Both are unusual. Sudden gusts of wind break or upend the native spruce, pine and alder trees rooted in the wet, unstable soil. After waiting out a storm, these windfalls become welcome sources of firewood to residents, but unfortunately casualties do sometimes occur to structures necessitating owners to repair damages. In January 1921, several violent storms battered the Washington coast. High tides combined with heavy rainfall caused flooding. The churning water weakened the jetty. The storm passed and, as usual, oceanside residents resumed their daily lives.

Fishing boats in the Marina are victims of the storm.

Always interesting, our weather, challenging, and when the sun smiles down, the beach is a most beautiful place to be. But out on the entrance to Grays Harbor off Chehalis Point, vessels, large and small, have been lost to sudden high winds and freak waves. Prior to the development of engines, the only control sailing ships had over their direction was a tiller and the maneuverability of their sails. If too close to shore during stormy weather, seamen would drop all of their anchors, but even this was not always effective against strong currents. Vessels were sometimes carried onto the shallow sand islands that build up from the silt forever drifting down the Chehalis River. During a storm, wooden ships were often safer out on the ocean, away from land, as their buoyancy allowed them to ride waves of considerable height.

Shipwreck Bounty

Early in its history, ship traffic in and out of American ports on all coastal waters caused the Federal government to take protective measures against the hazards brought on not only by nature but also by those engaged in piracy or smuggling. Beginning in 1790, a fleet of ten boats formed the Revenue Marine. It remained so-called until 1863 when it became the Revenue Cutter Service.

In his journal on March 23, 1865, Patterson Luark reports a shipwreck which occurred at the entrance to the Columbia River. Ten days later containers of flaxseed oil washed onto the beaches of Grays Harbor. He also wrote that "large quantities of whisky have been picked up by both whites and Indians and therefore all along the beach from the wreck northward to the straits of Fuca there is a general debauch in a certain class of humanity of both races."

Over the next few years, there were many shipwrecks both inside and outside of Grays Harbor, with at least ten schooners whose fates were determined in the shallow waters surrounding Chehalis Point: *Decatur* grounded in 1865, *Trustee* in 1886, *Big River* in 1892, *Nora Harkins* in 1894, *Fawn* in 1901, *Alcade* and *Emma Utter* in 1908, and *Balboa* in 1914. The barkentine *Monitor* foundered off the coast and the steam schooner *Wahkeena* stranded in the Harbor in 1929. Each of these ships no doubt deposited usable items on the beach for the benefit of Westport residents. In 1925, a Japanese ship lost a cargo of flour packed in waterproof bags which landed in many a Westport kitchen.

Saving Lives At Sea

Lifesaving Service Formed

In 1871 the Revenue Cutter Service increased its duties by giving aid to distressed vessels, forming the Lifesaving Service. Stations established along the Pacific coast included one at the south entrance to Grays Harbor. When that facility was opened in 1897, Charles Jacobsen became its first keeper. Jacobsen, one-time assistant keeper of the Shoalwater Bay Station at North Cove, was transferred from Point Adams station on the Columbia River to Peterson Point (Westport). When he moved, the youngest member of his family was a two-week-old son, Roy, known as "Sharkey" for most of his life.

Captain Charles Jacobsen and his crew lived at the United States Lifesaving Station shown in the center. (No names available)

The Lifesaving Station at the end of Ocean Avenue was opened in 1897. It became the United States Coast Guard Station in 1915.

Lifesaving crew with Captain Charles Jacobsen seated in the center.

The surf boat is manned by six oarsmen with the coxswain at the back steering with his "sweep."

Lifesaving crew stands in front of the boathouse with equipment used to bring stranded people to shore.

Crew practices on the beach using the breeches buoy method of lifesaving from ship to shore.

At the time the station was established, tidal waters reached much further inland along the ocean side of the Point. The Lifesaving Station, situated at the outer end of Ocean Avenue, included living quarters for personnel and a nearby building in which a thirty-six-foot surf boat was kept. When needed for rescue work, or for practice, the boat was drawn by horse across the sand to the water's edge and launched directly into the surf. A crew of six oarsmen manned the boat while a coxswain stood at the stern, steering with a eighteen-foot ash wood oar called a "sweep." The lifeboat was self-bailing and, should it roll over in rough seas, would right itself. Practice sessions on the sand dunes using the breeches buoy method of rescue offered a pleasant form of entertainment for the onlookers of Chehalis Point.

Charles Jacobsen commanded the station for twenty years during which time he took part in two hundred eighty-one rescue missions with no lives lost. Before he left in 1917, the Lifesaving Service became a Coast Guard facility. His duties as commander were taken over by his son, Roy. The Coast Guard Service was a part of the Department of Treasury except in times of war when it was directed by the United States Navy.

Signal Beacon Through The Night

As a further aid to navigation, lighthouses had been placed at the entrance to the Columbia River in 1856 and Shoalwater (Willapa) Bay in 1858, but not until 1893 was approval given by the Lighthouse Establishment for a light and fog signal building to be erected near the Lifesaving Station at Point Chehalis.

Designed by C. W. Leick, the project was approved in 1896 by Captain W. L. Fisk, Corps of Engineers Office of the thirteenth Lighthouse District, Portland, Oregon. The following year ground was broken for construction of the one hundred seven foot tower, the top of which still rises one hundred twenty-three feet above sea level. A contract was signed with Henry LePaute & Sons of Paris, France to supply the third Order Fresnel light, the platform on which it was to rest, and the 135 inside circular steps (originally lighted by windows) leading from the base to the top platform.

Though completion of the last ten feet of the tower was delayed for a short time, the light began its service on June 30, 1898. The turning mechanism, set in a drum of mercury, was cranked by hand each day to rotate the oil-fueled lamp. The light alternated red and white flashes from an hour before sunset to an hour after sunrise. The Grays Harbor light was visible for more than twenty-three miles in clear weather. The glass of the tower is 1/4" thick, its reflection a hazard to nearby vegetation if the window shades are not drawn during a sunny day. Later, when electricity was brought to Chehalis Point, a small motor eliminated the daily cranking chore, and a 1,000-watt light bulb replaced the need for lamp oil.

Grays Harbor Light at Westport was commissioned in 1898. The fog and signal building next to the lighthouse burned down in 1923.

A fog and signal house was placed next to the lighthouse. Its smokestack towered up to half the height of the light. When fog rolled in, the keeper had the unpopular task of hurriedly lighting a fire under the boiler to get enough steam to activate the horn, or the two trumpets, as they were called. Their eerie sound was used as a warning to ships that land was near.

Christian Zauner arrived at the new Grays Harbor Lighthouse on June 14, 1898 to become its first keeper. Zauner, born in Austria in 1855, came to the United States and settled in Oregon when he was a young lad. He acquired his U.S. citizenship in 1886, the same year he began his career in the Lighthouse Service.

He was appointed Second Assistant Keeper at the memorable Tillamook Rock Lighthouse five years after it opened. Three years later he was sent to the much more spacious lighthouse on Destruction Island as First Assistant. He became Keeper in 1895 and remained there until he was transferred to Grays Harbor as the first keeper of the new lighthouse. He salary was $800 a year with housing furnished for himself and his personnel.

The first Grays Harbor Light Keeper was Christian Zauner. Here he is shown with his wife, Hermina, and daughter, Mabel. Dorothy Zauner/Armstrong Collection.

When Christian Zauner married, he became the stepfather to Abigail, daughter of Hermina Zauner. He and Hermina, known as Mimi, had one daughter, Mabel. Mabel was married to Charles Armstrong, eldest son of Minnie and Ben Armstrong, whose Westport home is now a bed and breakfast known as Glenacres Inn. Mabel Armstrong died at age thirty-two, leaving three daughters; Dorothy, Lois and Mary Jane, in the care of family members. Widower Charles then met Jessie McKenzie while on a trip. They were married and became parents of two more daughters, Charlene and Betty.

Zauner had been keeper at the Grays Harbor Lighthouse for twenty years when the signal house caught fire and burned to the ground. A new lookout tower and fog signal building were built about a half-mile north of the station, with a long wooden walkway between the two structures. The lighthouse barracks that had been converted to a Coast Guard radio station was used for many years until it became obsolete and was razed in 1972. The present lookout tower located at the entrance to Westhaven State Park, displaying wind and storm signal flags was replaced in early 1996. The fog signal building between Half Moon Bay and the jetty was the victim of erosion in December of 1995 when the South Jetty was breached allowing free flow of water between the ocean and Half Moon Bay. It was not rebuilt as it was no longer needed.

A new fog signal was placed about a half-mile from the lighthouse and was lost to erosion before 1990. The radio beacons were dismantled when no longer used. Courtesy Jones Photo

A wooden walkway made travel easier between the station and fog horn building.

Flag on the modern lookout tower warns of wind velocity.

Christian Zauner retired in 1925 after thirty-nine years in the Lighthouse Service. J. Wilson, Assistant Keeper, took over the lighthouse operation until the next year when Arvil R. Settles assumed command. In 1935, Roy Jacobsen was appointed the last keeper and stayed in that position until the Coast Guard personnel took of the duties of the Lighthouse Service in 1939.

Zauner, at age eighty-eight, died in Westport in 1944. He was buried in Aberdeen with full military honors.

The Westport Card Club in 1910 consisted of Lifesaving Station and Lighthouse personnel and wives.

The residences of the Coast Guard Station when no longer in use were razed in the 1970s.

After the Pacific Avenue Dock had been built, the Coast Guard lifeboat was kept in a boathouse at the end of the dock and was lowered to the water by block and tackle.

Finding Safe Harbor

Jetties Built

The Harbor entrance, with its shifting sand, was in need of some kind of control to try to keep the Grays Harbor shipping channel open the year around to ocean-going vessels. In 1896 the U.S. Corps of Engineers began the enormous task of building a jetty from the ocean side of Chehalis Point out into the sea. Six years were to pass before its completion. Three years later the jetty on the north side of the Harbor was begun with nine years of construction bringing the work to a finish. Though the South Jetty did not last long, the two barriers did make passage safer for vessels coming into the Harbor.

By the beginning of the twentieth century, the lifesaving station, the lighthouse, and the jetties were all providing safety factors for the men who made their living on or from the sea. Wireless radios using the dots and dashes of the Morse Code made

Right: Captain Zauner at age seventy in 1925 when he retired after thirty-nine years of service. Dorothy Zauner/Armstrong Collection.

communication possible between ships and land. Engines were installed in boats, greatly increasing their mobility.

After the first motorized lifeboat arrived at Westport in 1914, the housing for the Lifesaving Surf Boat was moved from the sand dunes to a boathouse on the long wooden pier at the foot of Pacific Avenue, on the west side of Point Chehalis. The surf men responded to calls by driving the truck from Ocean Avenue to the dock where the surf boat was lowered into the water using chain blocks.

Port Formed & Harbor Dredging Begins

The citizens of Chehalis County voted their approval in December 1911 for the formation of the Port of Grays Harbor Organization. Ten years were to pass before the port commissioners made the decision to dredge the inner waters of Westport's harbor in hopes that the combination of jetties and dredging would keep the channel deep enough to allow large ships to reach the docks of businesses along its shores. For this work, the services of the dredge *Washington No. 4* were leased for two years. Realizing the need for frequent use, in 1923, the Port of Grays Harbor purchased the dredge from the Tacoma Dredging Company and renamed it *Robert Gray*. The 100-foot dredge successfully completed work around the Harbor for the next fifty-one years. Since then, dredging has been contracted out to private companies.

The United States Geologic survey map of Chehalis Point, dated 1913, shows one hundred thirty-three buildings, with the Lifesaving Lookout tower as the only structure in the Westhaven area. At that time, the land surrounding Westhaven was marshy and no road connected it with the town.

On June 16, 1914, the town called Peterson on Chehalis Point had its name officially changed to Westport.

In 1915 the Revenue Cutter and Lifesaving Services were combined, forming the United States Coast Guard Service. The existing Lifesaving Station near the lighthouse became the Coast Guard Station.

Bar Pilots Guide Ships

History shows that crossing the Grays Harbor bar prior to the construction of the jetties was indeed hazardous. Captains of ocean-going ships acknowledged the need for assistance and prevailed upon local owners of small boats familiar with Harbor waters to help them navigate through the channel. A lucrative business was born. As soon as a mast was sighted on the western horizon, a race was on between the skippers of the small boats to be the first to reach an incoming vessel. This confusion necessitated the forming of a company consisting of licensed pilots who would either tow the ships with their tugs or would board the ships and bring them in and out of the Harbor.

Despite all the precautions, there were still accidents to cope with. The 717 ton, four-masted schooner *King Cyrus*, built in 1890 by Hall Brothers of Port Blakely, made many trips carrying lumber from Grays Harbor. On July 17, 1922, the ship was returning from a trip to Honolulu when it suddenly lost control at the Harbor entrance.

The schooner *King Cyrus* was stranded on Westport's beach in 1922 and was a total loss except for items salvaged as it broke up.

Drifting free, the schooner became wedged onto a sand island. The tug *Cudahy*, standing by to tow it to port, immediately tried to pull the ship away from the sand bar but was unable to do so. An emergency call brought a second tug which also attached lines to the schooner. The two tugs could not free the *King Cyrus* from the grip of the sand. Finally, considered a total loss, the schooner was left to its fate, eventually breaking apart off the Westport shore. Many pieces of the *King Cyrus* were salvaged and are on display in the Shipwreck Room of the Westport Maritime Museum.

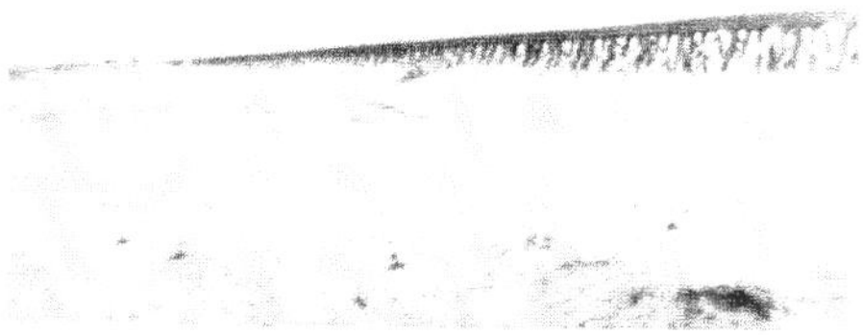

Rebuilding of the South Jetty began in 1935. A trestle for a railroad line started at a dock on the Harbor side and went across the Point to the edge of the ocean.

Sand Spit Builds

When the construction of a road made it possible to drive across the marshy land to the sandy point, Isom Channel opened a grocery store there in 1928. One year later the Port of Grays Harbor began to acquire land along the shore, now known as Westhaven. In 1930, 618 acres of waterfront land were offered to Ed Kaakinen of Kaakinen Fish Company, for $150, a goodly sum considering the depression times which had befallen the country. Kaakinen realized that millions of dollars he did not have nor could ever get, would have to be expended in order to make Westhaven a viable port. He refused the offer, the Port retained ownership and was later able to lease out much of the nearly one thousand acres they had acquired.

Engine No. 1204 made many trips pulling cars loaded with rock to the end of the jetty as it grew.

The Standard Oil bulk plant was added in 1930, managed by Leo Cournoyer. By now the physical beach line of Westport had changed due to construction of the South Jetty which created a build-up of land on the ocean side of the Point. Though the shoreline at the Point consisted mostly of tide flats, six buildings and a dock had been erected there. A section of driftwood-covered beach owned by Charles Yana, Frank Peterson and Harry Harms was sold for one dollar to the United States Government in 1935. This was to be the site of a new, larger Coast Guard Station. At the same time, the United States Corps of Engineers recognized the need to rebuild the crumbling jetties.

Jetties Rebuilt

The reparation project began in 1935. One of the first workers hired was James Empey of Aberdeen who arrived in August with his wife, Nellie, and nine-month-old son. Empey was put in charge of maintenance, primarily to keep machinery in good repair.

An office building was erected on a sand dune between the main part of the Town of Westport and the Westhaven Dock area. In the back of the building was a large concrete vault used for the safekeeping of papers and cash for workers' wages. The building, now a private residence, has the unique feature of an indestructible vault as part of the home. In the back yard of the house are traces of dugouts used during World War II, also a gun emplacement. There was a tunnel leading to the beach, later destroyed as a potential danger to the people of the community.

A huge barge, appropriately named the *Mastodon,* built in New York and too large to go through the Panama Canal, was towed around Cape Horn to Hoquiam. Massive rocks found in a Thurston County quarry were loaded onto flatcars and hauled by railroad to Hoquiam. On each trip the flatcars, up to twenty-one at a time, were moved onto the barge. The services of three tugs were needed to tow it across the Harbor to Westport. A pier for the *Mastodon* was located inside the Harbor entrance which helped to create a small cove. The pier was later used as a moorage place for local fishing boats.

A long line of flat cars loaded with rocks are pulled by railroad engine on the top of the growing jetty.

Two railroad trestles with tracks permitted the flatcars to move from the barge to the top of the developing jetty. A crane on the parallel track tipped the flatcars over, tumbling the rocks down the side of the wall. As the length of the jetty increased, more tracks were laid allowing the railroad engine to move outwards.

During the reparation, two men lost their lives and many injuries were treated. A near tragedy occurred when a locomotive engineer went into insulin shock and lost consciousness while holding the throttle wide open. The brakeman,

Double rows of tracks lengthen as the jetty is being built outward.

A steam engine picks up a rock ready to be pushed over the side of the trestle.

Aerial view of the Marina shows the railroad trestle tracks in the foreground.

who realized the train was not slowing as it should, was able to stop the engine when only seventy-five feet from the end of the unfinished jetty.

New Coast Guard Station

Work on the Coast Guard Station at its new location was also progressing. First consideration was that the building would need protection from tidal waters. This was solved by installing a border of interlocking steel plates along the entire edge of the property. The ground inside the bulkhead was filled so that it rose seventeen feet above high tide. A water-tight basement for the building was formed by two-foot thick concrete walls.

The white Nantucket-design building rises three stories above the basement, topped with a watchtower and widow's walk. The station with facilities for twenty officers and men was completed in 1939 and dedicated in 1940. A long boardwalk from the station extended into the bay and held a boathouse in which the Coast Guard lifeboat was kept. The end of the dock provided moorage space for other Coast Guard vessels. The building was finished at a cost of $52,500. The equipment shed next door and bulkhead surrounding the property added another $30,000 to the total price.

Hilman & Fridolf Persson

The Coast Guard Station in its new location is ready for occupancy in 1939.

While construction of the jetties and the station was underway, the Coast Guardsmen, under the command of Hilman Persson, continued to respond to distress calls as well as fulfilling other duties. Born in 1898, Persson had been brought to Grays Harbor by his brother, Mattis, who was a member of the original crew at the Lifesaving Station. Unable to speak English, Hilman was an eighteen-year-old in 1906 when he arrived in Westport. He worked at the station from 1907 to 1919 when he transferred to the Willapa Bay Lifesaving Station at North Cove. As an assistant there, he gained excellent experience, due to the off-and-on health of keeper Captain Herman Winbeck. When the keeper at Westport, Oscar Hawthorne, died in 1922, Persson was brought back to Westport to serve as Commanding Officer.

Fridolf Persson, son of Hilman and Eliza Armstrong Persson, wrote a brief history of his father's career as a Coast Guardsman.

Hilman Persson was an eighteen year old when he arrived from Sweden to begin his long career in the Coast Guard Service.

"The Coast Guard Cutter branch, which was, until World War II, totally separate from the Lifeboat Station branch, had a patrol boat stationed at each harbor up and down the coast. Its sole responsibility was to stop smuggling. When they went into dry dock for repairs, the Lifeboat Station had to take up the patrols. Most of the boats caught during prohibition were at this time. I suppose the smugglers thought they could get away with it when they saw the patrol boat on the way. Dad (Hilman Persson) caught several boat loads of whiskey coming in over the bar and a couple times the whiskey runners had already made the beach before they were caught.

"One time Dad got word there was a truck coming up from Tokeland headed for Aberdeen loaded with booze. Communications were slow and often times nonexistent, so the sheriff could not be notified. Dad took the crew in the truck and went down the road. They came upon the truck loaded with booze stuck in a mud hole, so that was another load confiscated in Dad's time. Just before Dad took charge of the Westport station when Mr. Hawthorne was in charge, a booze boat missed the Harbor entrance and came in on the beach. This boat was loaded with Canadian booze and Hawthorne, being a conscientious skipper as all of them were in those days, saw to it that every bottle of booze was broken. Canadian whiskey was hard to come by during prohibition and as prohibition was never popular with most people, it was kind of heart breaking to see bottle after bottle of Canadian whiskey broken into a trench and then buried."

Captain Persson was commanding officer of the Grays Harbor Station when one of the most dramatic rescues took place at the entrance to Willapa Bay, fifteen miles south of Grays Harbor. On May 7, 1937, winds up to sixty miles an hour had forced the 967-ton lumber schooner *Trinidad* off-course and the ship was swept onto the spit near North Cove. A flare from the ship was sighted by a lookout at the North Cove Lifeboat Station but its crew was at sea aboard its only boat, helping a fishing boat in distress. The duty officer called the Westport Station asking for assistance.

Captain Persson and four of his men boarded the thirty-eight foot Lifeboat No. 2839 and left Westport at 8 p.m. After a harrowing nine-hour trip on the stormy sea, they reached the battered *Trinidad*, but not before its second mate had been swept overboard and was lost. The Coast Guard lifeboat approached the ship on its sheltered side, using great caution, when it was discovered that the rigging from a broken mast was dangling over the side into the water, creating the danger of its lines becoming entangled in the wheel of the rescuing boat. A lifeboat from the deck of the *Trinidad* was carefully lowered but was immediately smashed.

The five Coast Guardsmen who rescued the crew of the *Trinidad* at North Cove in 1937. L-R: Ron Wood, Roy Anderson, Captain Hilman Persson, Jess Mathews and D. E. Hamalainan.

In spite of the turbulence surrounding them, the experienced Coast Guardsmen were able to take the men off the *Trinidad*, two or three at a time, until all twenty-one were crowded into Lifeboat No. 2839. A responding ship, the *Ruth E*, was standing by and the men were safely transferred to its deck. The body of the second mate surfaced in Grays Harbor several days later.

The rescue of the crew of the *Trinidad* was voted the most outstanding Coast Guard feat of 1937. The following year, Captain Persson and his crew, Roy L. Anderson, Jess W. Mathews, Ron N. Woods and D. E. Hamalainan each received a gold Congressional Medal in a ceremony aboard the Coast Guard Cutter *Onandaga* which came to Grays Harbor for that purpose. Captain Persson was later brought to Washington, D.C. where he was awarded the American Legion medal for valor. A detailed story about the stranding of the *Trinidad* was written by the late Betty Butler, a Westport resident who wrote for *The Daily World* in Aberdeen for many years.

Fridolf Persson signed on as a surfman at the Grays Harbor Station in 1938, the same year his father was transferred to the District Office in Seattle, keeping the tradition of having a Persson at the Westport Station since it was commissioned in 1897. The following year, 1939, the station was moved from Ocean Avenue to Westhaven Drive. Persson served there all through World War II during which time the Coast Guard recruited young men from the midwest and sent them to Westport, most of whom had never sailed or even seen the ocean. After the war ended, Fridolf Persson decided not to re-enlist.

A copy of Fridolf Persson's biographical sketch of his father's Coast Guard service is in the files of the Westport Maritime Museum.

South Jetty Rebuild Completed

The South Jetty, now extending two and a half miles into the sea, was finished in 1939. The construction of the jetty on the north side of the Harbor entrance began that year and was completed in 1942.

The South Jetty at Westport in place by 1939.

James Empey stayed in Westport until the South Jetty was in place. He and his family moved to Aberdeen in 1939 but returned six years later to make Westport their permanent home. Eventually four more sons and one daughter joined the family.

Nellie Empey went on to work in the first fishing charter office at Westport and later held positions in various business stores until she retired at the end of 1994. James Empey died in 1979. Nellie Empey has been a volunteer in the Westport Maritime Museum for several years.

Shipping Traffic On The Harbor

Since their installation in 1867, channel markers leading into Grays Harbor have required constant attention because of weather conditions. Over the years, several types of buoys have been created to guide vessels safely into port. Some of these markers resemble miniature floating lighthouses. The first buoys with lights were fueled with oil, the supply of which had to be replenished regularly. This was the job held by Hoquiam resident, Oscar Stensager, in 1934 when he became a Light Attendant for the Lighthouse Service. He had his own boat in which he brought oil to the buoys within Grays Harbor and on the rivers emptying into same. Stensager also took care of other maintenance as needed. He retired in 1964 after completing thirty years of government service.

Ships, called buoy tenders, to take care of lights and markers in the outer channels, had been in existence since the early 1900s. They were crewed by seamen who did the servicing, cleaning and relocating of the buoys. The Coast Guard Service became responsible for the maintenance of all channel markers in 1939 after they assumed duties of the Lighthouse Service.

Coast Guard Tender *Fir* serviced the buoys in Washington State coastal waters for fifty years. She was retired in 1991.

At the outbreak of World War II, channel lights were extinguished for protection from the enemy, a challenge to those who found themselves out on the sea and approaching land at night.

Battery-operated lights have long since replaced the need for fuel oil, but the tenders are always busy. The *Heather*, based in Astoria, fulfilled these duties in Grays Harbor waters for many years. The aging ship was replaced by the *Fir* which was launched in California in 1939, one month before the Lighthouse Service became part of the Coast Guard Service.

The buoy tender *Fir* completed fifty years of service along the Columbia River, the Washington coast, the Strait of Juan de Fuca and Puget Sound. When in the Grays Harbor area, the *Fir* was able to dock at Westhaven Cove after the basin had been dredged. When the *Fir* was retired in 1991, its duties were taken over by the *Iris*. Also based in Astoria, Oregon, the *Iris* currently tends the markers leading into Grays Harbor.

Corps Cuts A Channel

Another frequent visitor to Westport from 1937 on was the United States Corps of Engineers Survey Boat *Mamala*. Built in Seattle in 1931, the crew of the *Mamala* surveyed Hawaiian Island waters for six years, then was transferred to Seattle to work in the harbors of the Washington coast. The sixty-five foot motorship, with a crew of two and a survey crew of three, was equipped with a depth finder and radar. Whenever soundings showed Grays Harbor channels were becoming clogged with sand, the crew of the *Mamala* alerted the dredge *Robert Gray* that its services were needed. During the stay in Grays Harbor, the *Mamala* was moored at Westhaven Cove. The boat retired from service in 1992 and is presently docked at Hoquiam.

The *Shoalhunter*, built in Tacoma in 1993, is stationed in Willapa Bay and at Westport when in Grays Harbor. Skippered by Tom Landreth, this sophisticated fifty-eight-foot vessel is equipped with devices to measure depth and computer printout capabilities. The boat is designed similar to a purse seiner and can troll for fish to test time elements best suited for dredging.

The Corps of Engineers Survey Boat *Mamala* was retired to Hoquiam in 1992 after thirty-five years of sounding Grays Harbor.

Two World Wars

Effects Of War on Westport

The entrance of the United States into World War I in 1917 was centered in the European area and did not have much effect on the Town of Westport, population of about two hundred persons. There was a small barracks to house the soldiers who came to build and man gun emplacements dotted around the South Beach sand dunes. The soldiers had horses for local transportation and kept them in a nearby pasture. Never necessary, the gun emplacement sites were abandoned.

A young lady sits on the end of a World War I weapon at one of the gun emplacements overlooking the Grays Harbor entrance.

During World War II, soldiers on horseback patrolled the beach from Westport to North Cove until there was no longer any threat of invasion.

It was a different matter when Hawaii's Pearl Harbor was bombed on December 7, 1941, as the Pacific coastline was now vulnerable to attack by the Japanese Navy. World War II caused much disruption in the lives and activities of the people of Westport. The United States Army immediately sent soldiers to guard the beaches and the port. They were housed throughout the area wherever space was available. More gun emplacements were added to the old ones. A temporary station was set up by the Coast Guard at the site of the present Lamplighter Restaurant in Grayland. All outside lights were extinguished at night, causing great difficulty for the Coast Guard personnel when they responded to distress calls. In at least one instance, the soldiers guarding the shore mistakenly fired upon a Coast Guard lifeboat returning to port. Fortunately, no one was hurt by the friendly fire.

When months passed without invasion from enemy forces, most of the soldiers were relocated, some to work on a highway through Canada to Alaska, some to join combat forces in the South Pacific.

Boats were recruited for patrol duty on the waters of Grays Harbor.

A crash boat was based at the Coast Guard Station dock in Westport.

Coast Guard Barge In Westport

During World War II, the U.S. Coast Guard at Westport had a large barge which was located on the northeastern side of the 620 foot pier. The barge was equipped with living quarters for four to six Coast Guardsmen who worked 48 hours on shift and 48 hours off. Local resident, Dorothy Warford, recalls that her husband, Hugh W. Warford, a Seaman 1st Class in the Coast Guard during the war years, was transferred to Westport for duty on the barge in early 1945.

"The small cadre seemed to be completely separate from the Coast Guard Station, although my husband, who cooked aboard the barge, reported that he and his fellow crew members got their stores from the big walk-in freezers and refrigerators in the main station's galley, along with all the other supplies they needed. The only access to the barge was by rowboat, and sometimes in bad weather, the water was very rough."

Immediately prior to being stationed in Westport, Warford was stationed at the hotel at Copalis Beach and served as a cook for the Beach Horse Patrol and those assigned to the bunkers on the north shore.

The job of those assigned to the barge was to log incoming and outgoing fishing vessels, recording departure and arrival times and noting in which direction the boats were going (north banks or south banks). Warford reported that the fishermen grumbled regularly about having to check in and out, because they were convinced that the Coast Guardsmen were spying on where they were catching fish and telling other fishermen.

According to Warford, "When the boats had all gone out in the morning, time was heavy on the fellows' hands, so oftentimes they did odd jobs around town like mowing lawns, digging clams for sale to restaurants in town, picking blackberries to sell, etc. They also worked at the commercial fisherman's warehouse on the dock, unloading catch as the boats returned, because there was always a shortage of workers.

"On Saturday nights, a big poker game was held aboard the barge with the fishermen joining the crew. Hugh, who was no gambler, always had a sure thing. He earned $3 for furnishing coffee and sandwiches to the players, which supplemented his regular Coast Guard pay of $13 every two weeks ."

When the barge was decommissioned several months after Warford was assigned to it, the men were instructed to throw everything overboard, which they did. Warford was then transferred to Mukilteo to guard an ammunition dump, and the barge continued to serve the commercial fishing industry at the main dock.

Also of interest is the fact that a similar barge was placed on Willapa Harbor during the war years. When it was decommissioned after the war, it found a new life as an extremely popular eatery located on the southern outskirts of Raymond and appropriately named The Barge Restaurant. The original barge was recently replaced.

Fishing Fleet Demands Expand

Marina Development

The first major dredging to make a basin at Westport began in 1942 when the *Robert Gray* came to deepen the cover. The dredged sand was emptied onto the beach, but lack of bulkheads caused it to filter back into the bay. However, the basin was now large enough to hold the Coast Guard pier at one side, Float 10 at the other side, and a 620-foot pier extending out into the water from Dock Street between the two. With these improvements, the dock at the foot of Pacific Avenue began its demise.

After World War II ended in 1945, the fishing industry took on a new importance for the people of Westport. Moorage space along the main pier was adequate for forty-seven boats but there was as yet no frontage road, no ramp and no boat hoist. The following year, more sand was dredged. In conjunction with that project, some bulk heading was done along the shore.

A storm in January 1950, brought high winds from the east blowing enough loose sand from the shore to close off the entrance to the cove. Again, the *Robert Gray* was sent for and 250,000 cubic yards of sand were removed, this time deposited on the inland marshes. About four hundred acres of property averaging a depth of three feet were created for the Port by the project.

By the end of the 1940s, the number of fishermen, both commercial and sport, supplied enough customers to keep two stores open for business on the dock. There were also two fish-packing plants, a tavern, a restaurant, fourteen small residences and four other buildings.

The potential of Westhaven Cove to become an important fishing port was brought to the attention of U.S. Congressman Russell W. Mack who, in turn, was able to get $675,000 from the government with which to start construction of a badly needed breakwater. Work on this project began May 1, 1950. When finished, a pair of rock and piling walls in the water formed a passageway for vessels to move in and out of the marina.

In order to stabilize the shoreline of the cove, creosoted pilings were installed along its edge and the space behind the wall was filled with 37,000 tons of rock. The exposed beach west of the cove behind the revetment, up to then reached only by boat or by foot at low tide, was leveled off. It created access to the point of sand that curved around the north end of the cove. Six groins extended into the water from the revetment in order to curb the currents.

In 1952 the main pier extending out into the bay from Dock Street was rebuilt with pilings treated for protection against the saltwater. The bulkhead to the west of the pier was finished. Dredging material was added behind that wall resulting in an improved Front Street. During 1955, after storm drains had been installed below ground, a new parking lot took care of the ever-increasing vehicle visits. PUD power was extended out to the floats for the convenience of the fishing fleet. The beach east of the Coast Guard pier still consisted of the original tide flats until 1956 when

The Coast Guard boathouse was at the end of a dock in front of the Station next to a fishing boat dock. In the background are the breakwaters which were installed in the 1950s.

Breakwater "C" was installed. This made it possible to tame the east end of the basin. Fire hydrants were added in 1957 after the water supply system was extended to Westhaven.

It was at this time that the need for a marina manager was taken care of. Leo Cournoyer, former manager of the Standard Oil bulk plant, whose position was filled by Martin Thurman, was appointed by the Port of Grays Harbor. The manager was at first given living quarters next door to a small building which served as an office. The house on Lamb Street was later turned into a larger office and the small building was used for storage. Cournoyer was followed by Lewis Caldwell who remained in that position until 1975 when former Coast Guardsman, James Whalen, managed the Port's interests in Westport for the next fifteen years. Larry Ivy served as Port Manager from 1990 to 1995, when he was transferred to Aberdeen. Ron Rausch is his successor.

An aerial scene which looks northwest from the Marina.

An aerial scene which looks southeast from the Marina.

The revetment wall protects Westport from tidal action. Across the entrance to Grays Harbor is Point Brown and the North Jetty.

Between 1950 and 1962 the Corps of Engineers spent more than two million dollars to create a safe harbor for Westport vessels. The Port's expenses were also great but when Floats 2, 4 and 6 were added to the northwest side of the main dock, and eight floats were added on the southeast side, these became a source of revenue from moorage fees. Docking capabilities were increased to five hundred eighty-three berths plus sixty-three private spaces. Front Street was regraded, paved and renamed Westhaven Drive.

The property in Westhaven held by the Port of Grays Harbor was extensive, considering the 2,000,000 cubic yards of sand that had been dredged from the cove and used for fill. Some of the land became available to use for businesses and parcels were leased on a ninety-nine year basis. The Port Commissioners, however, did not want to be in the rental business. In 1964 they presented a plan to sell the uplands. Their vote gave approval and Port began to sell off land at a gradual pace, adding the new private property owners to the county tax rolls.

Much of the information on the development of the dock area, prior to 1970, was compiled by Murray Fuller for the City of Westport. An undated draft of his report is kept at Westport City Hall.

In the 1960s several severe storms hit the Washington coast. One was the infamous Columbus Day Storm of 1962. Its one-hundred-plus miles per hour winds did much destruction to the entire Pacific Northwest. The jetties were not spared and again needed reinforcement. This was taken care of in 1966.

A different type of equipment was used when the jetty was repaired in 1966. The wall was made higher and was shortened. The end of the former jetty lies submerged and boats are warned of the hazard at low tide.

Piloting Ships To Shore

Once the practice of using pilots to bring large ships into Grays Harbor was firmly established, vessels were able to move in and out of the Harbor with greater safety. For many years the *M/V America*, a former halibut schooner built in 1910, was owned and operated by the Ocean Pilot and Tugboat Company. The *America* was bought in 1930, had a diesel engine installed in 1938, and was sold in 1945.

The Grays Harbor Pilots Association was formed in the late 1970s. Its structure was based upon the system adopted by the Columbia River Bar Pilots Association of Astoria, Oregon.

In 1977, the pilot boat *Columbia*, which had been in use on the Columbia River for almost twenty years, was purchased by Twin Harbors Launch Service, Inc., a company owned by the Grays Harbor Bar Pilots Association. The boat was refurbished and, when ready for service in Grays Harbor, was renamed *Chehalis*. The *Charleston Pilot* was added in September, 1980 and became *Grays Harbor*. Both vessels were upgraded in 1988.

The two pilot boats are based in Westport. Two men form the crew on each boat. When an incoming ship requests a pilot, one of the boats brings a licensed pilot to meet the ship out at sea. The pilot must them climb a ladder from the boat to the ship's

The rebuilt Westport Dock is a busy place.

The Pilot Boat *Chehalis* is moored in Westhaven Marina when not in service.

deck. The captain of the ship turns control over to the pilot who directs the helmsman across the bar to the proper dock. When the ship is ready to leave port, the pilot directs it out across the bar, followed by the pilot boat. The pilot climbs down the ladder from the ship and boards the pilot boat which brings him back to Westport. Many hazards to ships entering and leaving Grays Harbor have been alleviated thanks to the harbor pilots who performed this often precarious service.

Communications Lifeline

Josie Dyas On The Air

The seagoing populace of Grays Harbor gained another valuable service in water safety when Josephine Dyas came to Westport. Married in 1964, Josie and her husband, Ken lived in Tacoma and worked at St. Joseph Hospital for several years. With ocean fishing being the main attraction, they and their two young sons traveled to Westport in their motor home almost every weekend. Eventually Josie and Ken bought property near Lake Chehalis (commonly called "Fake Lake" by locals) on which they built their home.

Josie Dyas with her husband, Ken, has made Westport her home and spends much of her time by her radio giving assistance to anyone having problems at sea. *The Daily World* Photo.

One day when Josie and Ken were about forty miles offshore in their fishing boat *Jodya* (an appropriate combination of their names), Ken found a way to encourage Josie to learn how to use the technical equipment installed on the boat. In case of an accident to Ken, she would have to know how to call for help and to bring the boat safely back to port. Out of this necessity, Josie became familiar with and accomplished at using navigational instruments such as radio, radar, depth finders and compass. Little did either of them know how this knowledge would develop into a full time occupation.

The outside of the Dyas home, decorated with electronic equipment makes an interesting skyline.

Ken Dyas retired in the 1970s. Josie gave up her nursing job at the hospital and they moved to Westport, making it their permanent home. Ken fished commercially for several years and served as deputy sheriff. Josie had brought with her some of their communications equipment. In time, she filled their home not only with radios and the constant reminder of their presence, but also the technical tools used in gathering weather information for the National Oceanic and Atmospheric Administration (NOAA). This she does four times a day, seven days a week, using apparatus furnished by NOAA, the only employment for which she receives compensation.

Josie Dyas is able to receive and transmit messages to vessels out on the sea, mostly between Astoria, Oregon and the Strait of Juan de Fuca. Local fishermen know that if they become trapped in a fog bank or their boats are in functional distress, they can call "Jodya" (her CB nickname or "handle") for help. Whenever expedient, information received is relayed by her to the Coast Guard Station in Westport. Due to unusual weather conditions, she has received calls from as far away as Texas, California and Hawaii. One recent distress call came over the air from a fisherman who was concerned that his boat was taking on water after hitting an iceberg. A puzzled Josie finally got his location which was out at sea from his home port in Cordova, Alaska. Josie called the Coast Guard Station in Westport who contacted their station in Alaska. The boat and occupant were returned safely to port in Cordova.

One harrowing experience kept Josie at her radio for almost forty-four hours. Two fishing boats were caught in a storm one hundred and fifty miles from Westport. Winds were clocked at sixty miles an hour with swells of thirty feet. Because a determined Josie Dyas was able to talk them in, the two boats made it back to port safely.

Josie always works closely with the U.S. Coast Guard Service and has taken part in their practice rescues. She has gone on the Coast Guard helicopter in emergencies, her nurse's training put to good use. For the service she performs, the walls of the Dyas home are filled with awards and mementos from grateful recipients of her search and rescue efforts. She has received no less than four Meritorious Commendations from the United States Coast Guard.

The two retirees, Josie and Ken Dyas, continue to serve the community of Westport. The exterior of their home stands out with its unique decoration of sophisticated antennae necessary to perform this priceless lifesaving service. In the summer of 1997, grateful fisher folk and community members replaced the Dyas antenna tower with a new one.

Coast Guard On The Move

Another New Coast Guard Station

With the steady growth of water traffic in and out of Grays Harbor, additional Coast Guard personnel were needed to handle problems caused not only by unexpected storms but by inexperienced seagoers. By 1971, fifty men were stationed in a building meant to house twenty. Personnel stationed in Westport found living quarters wherever available, usually renting small homes, cottages or motel space. The two large houses on Ocean Avenue formerly used by the old Lighthouse personnel were turned over to the Coast Guardsmen and their families for recreational centers. The time had come for a larger facility to keep up with the needs of the Westport Coast Guard Station.

The much larger United States Coast Guard Station Grays Harbor at Westport was commissioned in 1973.

Land selected for the new structure sat at the east end of the dock area. It offered ample room for a large red brick building and enclosed boat house on the water, space enough for three lifeboats, a surf rescue boat, and an inflatable boat. The new station was commissioned in 1973 while Keith Herrell was Commanding Officer. The two wooden buildings on Ocean Avenue, no longer needed, were dismantled to make room for new housing for families of men stationed at the facility.

Maritime Museum Aborning

The Port of Grays Harbor owned the property on which the new station was erected. The Port traded the land for ownership of the Nantucket-style former Coast

Guard Station on Westhaven Drive. Orville Engle, one-time mayor, city councilman and owner of Sourdough Lil's Restaurant adjacent to the old station, considered the building an ideal site for a maritime museum. Engle approached the Port of Grays Harbor with a request that it donate the building to the city of Westport. He received no response and there definitely was not enough money in the city coffers to pay about $500,000 for the valuable grounds.

Three unsuccessful attempts to obtain the fine old building and its grounds had been made when mayor Bill Wade appointed Orville Engle to head a local Bicentennial Committee honoring the 1776 birth of the United States. The committee went after the building and finally the Port agreed to accept a one-dollar-a-year lease on it.

The station was renamed "Westport Marine Center" and was supported by a non-profit organization, the Friends of the Westport Marine Center. In order to raise money, many activities such as dances and rummage sales were held. Proceeds from those efforts enabled the Friends to match funds from the State Bicentennial Commission. The building was painted inside and out, all by donated labor.

In order for the city to buy the building without using tax money, some of the rooms were leased out as a source of income, done with the approval of the Port. Washington State Department of Fisheries became the first paying tenant, followed

Since 1985, the Nantucket-style former Coast Guard Station has been the home of the Westport Maritime Museum.

by the Westport Chamber of Commerce. Municipal Court cases were also heard there.

Orville Engle received an alarming bit of news when he learned that a woman from Alaska had offered to buy the station with the intention of using the upstairs rooms for her residence and the main floor for commercial purposes. Tempting as it was, the Port rejected the offer and finally decided to sell the building to the City of Westport for $100,000. The voters of Westport approved, on September 21, 1976, a bond issue of $107,000. The bond covered the building's purchase and necessary repairs. In March 1978, the Old Coast Guard Station was listed on the Washington State Register of Historic Places.

During the next few years non-profit groups took advantage of the space. Washington Trollers Association Auxiliary held meetings there. Boy Scout troops, 4-H Clubs, Senior Citizens and Alcoholics Anonymous all have been able to gather in its rooms free of charge.

When the Westport-South Beach Historical Society was formed in 1984, the building was turned over to its members for use as a maritime museum. A glass-walled whale house containing skeletons of whales, a sea lion and a porpoise was added to the grounds in 1986, a second one a few years later.

In celebration of the Washington State Bicentennial in 1989, a scale model replica of the original Cape Cod-style Coast Guard Station that now houses the museum was donated by General James H. Doolittle South Beach VFW Post No. 3057. Local Post member, Vic Nordloh, an accomplished carpenter and cabinet maker, spent thousands of hours researching creating the exact replica. Other post and auxiliary members created historically accurate furnishings for the interior. A duck boat display is a 1997 addition to the whale house.

With the help of a grant, the old fire station next door to the museum was remodeled. It is now the Westport Maritime Hall and is used for community functions, such as seminars by Dr. John Smith during the spring, on the migration of the gray whale. Historical Society meetings are also held there.

Orville Engle lived long enough to see the Westport Maritime Museum become a reality. He was a charter member of the Historical Society. In 1990, he died in Olympia.

Added to the grounds are two glass-walled buildings featuring skeletons of sea mammals, a duck boat display of items and photos from earlier years, as well as a scale model replica of the former Coast Guard station.

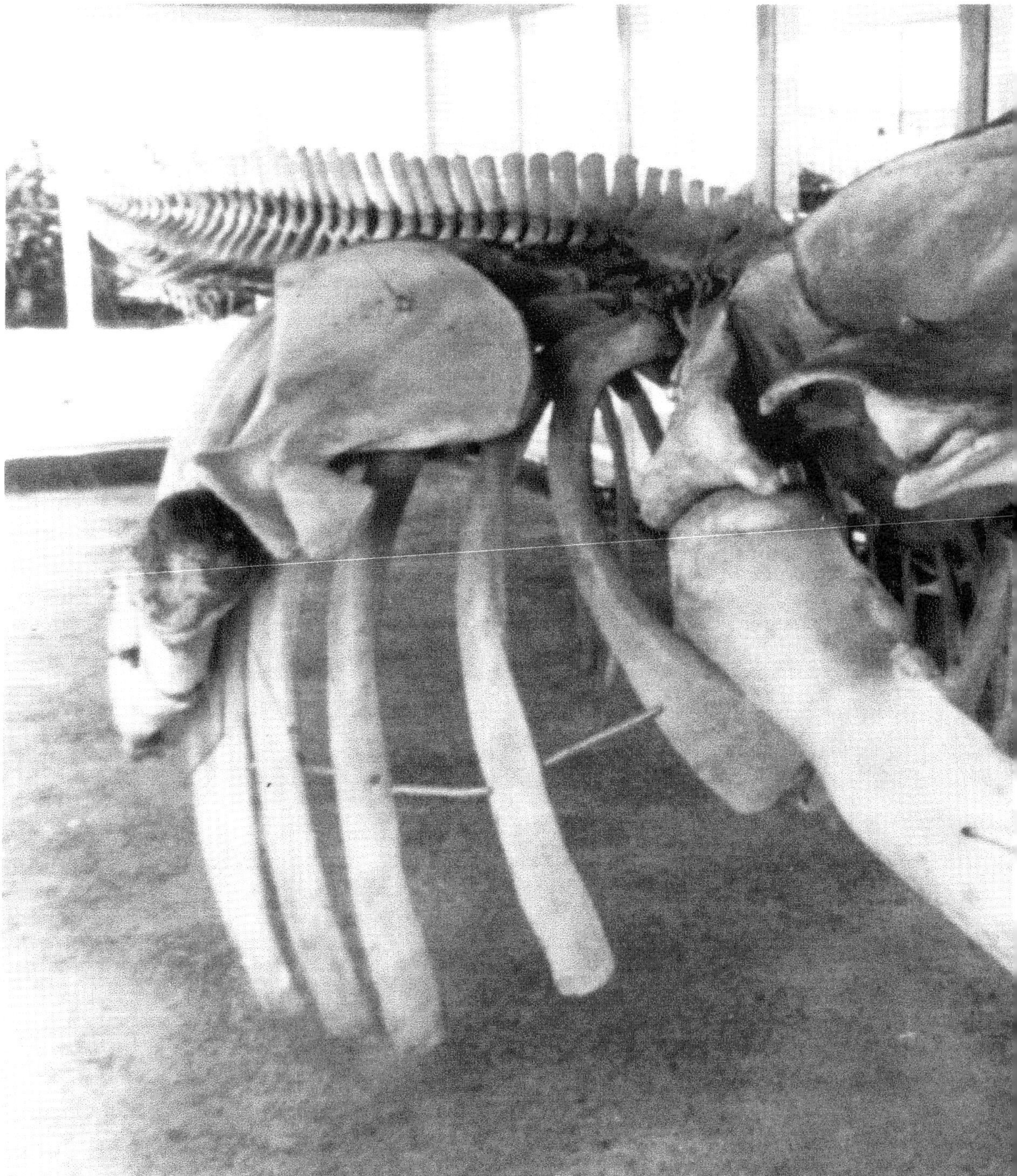

PART III

The Town Grows

What's In A Name?

Frank Millard Peterson, the only child of Jane and Glenn Peterson, was born in Portland, Oregon Territory, on March 21, 1855. On August 10, 1858, the family came to Chehalis Point and took over Thompson and Sophia Speake's claim. When all the original settlers had drifted off to other places, the Petersons remained on the Point which was to become their permanent home. Between 1861 when the fort closed and the 1870s, Chehalis Point lost all its non-native residents with the exception of the three-member Glenn Peterson family.

By the time he was twelve years old and interest was being revived in the area, Frank Peterson began hauling freight and passengers by wagon along the beach at low tide between Chehalis Point and North Cove, a distance of more than twenty miles.

Frank Peterson came to Chehalis Point at age three with his parents, Jane and Glenn Peterson. He and Mary Ann Tanger of Ilwaco were married in 1887. The Petersons were the only members of the original settlers to stay permanently on Chehalis Point.

By the time he was fifteen years old, he was serving as an interpreter between the Indian agent at Taholah and the local Indians among whom he had lived and from whom he had learned the language.

As an adult he held the contract for postal service and carried mail and freight around the Harbor in the *Maud K*, a thirty-four foot plunger (sloop) built by William Kindred of Tokeland. Over the years, Frank developed the original claim into a large productive piece of property. The Peterson home facing Grays Harbor was often used as a stopping place for travelers passing through the area.

Carl Tanger, who was first mate on a German sailing vessel, had visited Shoalwater (Willapa) Bay in the 1850s and never gave up his dream of some day returning to its shores. In the meantime, he married Irish immigrant Bridget Judge, with whom he had three daughters and one son. The Tangers lived for a time in Illinois until they decided to move west. A train took the family from Illinois to San Francisco where they boarded a vessel which sailed to Shoalwater Bay. They filed a claim on the Naselle River but gave it up when forty-four-year-old Carl Tanger drowned in 1873. Bridget Tanger moved to Oysterville where a fourth daughter was born eight months after her father's death. Bridget later married a widower, Marshall Soames, and the new family settled on a claim near Ilwaco.

One of the Tanger daughters, Mary Ann, was married to Frank Peterson on July 6, 1887. They had one son, Millard, who lived most of his life in and around the South Beach area. When Millard married, he acquired two stepchildren and then had one daughter, Elizabeth.

In 1879, another community south of Olympia on the Chehalis River had been officially recognized by the Washington State Legislature as "Chehalis." To avoid confusion for the postal service as well as everyone else , the town of Chehalis Point took the name "Peterson" for its mailing address.

By now, the newly-named town of Peterson had begun its recovery and people were moving back to Chehalis Point. Within five years, by 1884, there was enough interest in the area for Frank Peterson, Hilda McIntosh, and Lela Shute to plat a section of land southwest of the Point. Also known as part of the Town of Peterson, it was later renamed "Cohassett." On the Harbor side of the Point, Peterson and his wife platted that area as "Westport Beach" in 1891, later dropping the Beach.

Frank knew almost everyone, and everyone knew who he was. He had a phenomenal memory and loved to recount his early days on the Harbor. Unfortunately, there is no evidence of any of his experiences being recorded.

His parents, Jane and Glenn Peterson, were buried in the Oysterville Cemetery. Mary Ann Peterson died in 1922. Twenty years later, when Frank was eighty-seven years old, he suffered a heart attack, temporarily improving in a rest home. His heart gave out on June 5, 1942. Mary Ann and Frank Peterson are buried side by side in the Ilwaco Cemetery.

Hotels & Cottages Welcome Guests

People were fully dressed according to the style of the times, when walking the beach.

Westport Hotel

It was here, in Westport, that Charles W. Yana opened his Westport Hotel. When the Harbor steamer arrived at the dock at the foot of Pacific Avenue, guests were met by Yana in a fringe-topped surrey and brought to his hotel. On the up-to-date premises, furnishings such as handsome curtains imported from England graced the rooms. As there was no indoor plumbing at the time, wash bowls and pitchers on marble-topped commodes were available in each room, as well as lidded pots for emergency night time use.

Charles Yana built his Westport Hotel shortly before the turn of the last century.

A bridal suite dominated the second floor, on occasion used by newlyweds. The Westport Hotel, fairly easy to get to considering the times, became a popular lodging place for visitors to the coast. While vacationing there, some of the guests discovered ocean fishing, some dug clams, others beachcombed while walking the shoreline.

Walsh Addition

Aberdeen banker C. T. Wooding became involved in developing the area south of Peterson with beach cottages for summer use. Led by him, a group from Aberdeen arrived at the Westport dock on June 18, 1891 and were brought to Yana's Westport Hotel for the night. In the morning the guests were taken through the woods to look over sixty-four lots platted in the Walsh addition to the Town of Peterson. Fifty-nine lots were sold the first day. Within ten days, fourteen of them showed beginnings of cottages.

Pinehurst Hotel

A. D. Wood, a mill owner in Aberdeen, was one of the newcomers. He built Pinehurst Cottage which later became a hotel operated by his wife, Molly. Because of the geographic similarity between that location and a resort town on Massachusetts Bay, Molly Wood, who had lived at both places, instigated the renaming of that section of Peterson to "Cohassett."

Rooms at the Pinehurst Hotel in Cohassett cost $2 per day or $10 a week with special rates for families. The hotel had neither running water nor electricity. Fuel for the fireplaces was supplied from driftwood on the beach. Children under twelve years of age ate meals in their own separate dining room. Bathing suits to wear while playing in the ocean were rented for twenty-five cents. Near the beach was a bathhouse in which guests could wash off with saltwater heated on a wood burning stove.

Mrs. Wood ran the hotel for four years, then sold the property to the H. B. Waldrons. Allowing Wood's hotel to revert back to Pinehurst Cottage, Waldron built a new three-story hotel on the dunes, added a water tank with pump to supply running water, and named it the Essex Hotel.

A shipwreck had left a large supply of railroad ties that floated onto the beach. From these, Waldron constructed an unusual house for his family on the nearby sand dunes. There is said to have been a second building but the larger of the two was clearly visible from the ocean. Vessels used the "tie house," as it was called, as an aid to navigation when entering Grays Harbor. The two story house was shown on United States Coast and Geodetic Survey charts for years, long after it was destroyed by fire in the 1930s.

Essex Hotel

A car full of visitors comes through the gate at Cohasset, circa 1900.

Guests of the Essex Hotel were welcomed to the Cohassett development in the early 1900s.

The Essex Hotel was the social center of Cohassett and in 1909 became the location of the Cohassett Post Office with Waldron as postmaster. Horse-drawn carriages transported hotel guests across the sand dunes for those who wished to relax on the beach. The hotel flourished until about 1915 when it burned down. That and the onset of World War I caused a decline in the resort era of Cohassett Beach, leaving Pinehurst Cottage settled intact among the other residences.

In 1901 a sailing ship was wrecked off the coast with much of its cargo landing on Westport's shore. Charles Yana salvaged a huge wooden crate by using his draft horses to drag it two miles across the sand to his hotel. The well-packed crate contained a carved rosewood Chickering grand piano in excellent condition. The piano was put in the sitting room of the Westport Hotel and for many years filled the air with music by anyone who could play.

When Charles Yana died in 1935, one of the stipulations in his will was that "the piano must never be removed from these premises as long as this building stands." The Widow Yana sold the hotel to Katherine and Claude Messick, who did extensive improvements to the building.

When reopened again in 1937, there were eight bedrooms on the second floor and two more over the dining room. Two apartments were created out of a small house at the rear of the hotel. The Messicks used the original dining room for their living quarters. A wing added to the north side of the building became the new dining room. The former bar was remodeled into the register office. Bathrooms with showers were installed on both floors.

The South Jetty was being rebuilt at the time and work crews took their meals at the hotel. Some of the fifty men also rented sleeping rooms there. The Messicks raised their own meat and had staples brought by truck from Aberdeen. Breakfasts of bacon, eggs and pancakes were served in three shifts: 4 a.m., 6 a.m., and 8 a.m. Mrs.

The automobile was put into the garage at the Essex Hotel where it was safely kept until its next outing.

One of the cottages of Cohassett was used as a summer home.

Three brave souls venture into the surf at Cohassett Beach.

Messick packed lunches for the men and also did all of their laundry. Dinner was served family style. Charge for the use of the hotel facilities was $3 per day.

Two months after World War II was declared on December 8, 1941, Army personnel moved into Westport. The Messicks were ordered to evacuate the hotel so its rooms could be used by servicemen. Upon leaving Westport, they were assured everything would be well taken care of in their absence. The Messicks moved to Puyallup for the duration. When they returned to Westport after the War, they found the hotel in shambles, never to be restored. Its paneling had been removed, the linoleum gone, furniture damaged and mattresses taken by soldiers out to the sand dunes on night duty.

The piano, which had been uncovered was destroyed beyond repair. The ivory was torn from the keys, the strings were cut and cigarette burns dotted the once-beautiful rose-wood covering. No explanation was given to the heart-broken Messicks. Ralph Boohm bought the hotel in 1957, removed what materials he could, then had the building razed.

Armstrong Family & Mill

When James Swan wrote his *Northwest Coast* about the three years he lived at Shoalwater (Willapa Bay), he made mention of Benjamin C. Armstrong and his famous lumber mill. Armstrong was twenty-seven years old when he crossed the country by wagon train, settling near Grays Harbor in 1852. He and two partners cut a trail to Cedar Creek near the present town of Oakville. The creek supplied a natural source of power from a waterfall which made it an ideal place on which to build the first sawmill in Chehalis County. Patterson Luark bought lumber from the mill as did the James family and most of the other area pioneers.

Ben Armstrong and Mary Nechard, daughter of the Chief of the Satsop Tribe, were married in 1855. Two years later, Armstrong was found dead under mysterious circumstances. The thirty-two-year-old mill operator had died five months before his third child was born on February 7, 1858.

As a full-blooded Indian, Mary Armstrong was legally prevented from claiming her husband's property. It was put under control of estate managers who confiscated most of the Armstrong assets. The three children of Ben and Mary—Charles, Julia, and Ben Jr.—were placed in foster homes. Mary eventually became the wife of Captain John Riddell of Bruceport on Shoalwater Bay. He did what he could to help the children claim some of their rightful inheritance. However, the Armstrong mill burned down and was a total loss.

Young Ben Armstrong ran away from his foster home and worked in Northwest logging camps during his growing years. He and Minnie Ross Smith, formerly of Nova Scotia, were married in 1888. The next nineteen years produced seven children

Benjamin Franklin Armstrong survived his childhood, took possession of land in Westport on his father's claim, and built a large home for his family. Dorothy Zauner/Armstrong Collection.

as well as a small fortune through the logging business. The family moved to Westport and in 1908 regained the land claimed by Ben's father in 1851 for their future home. A sixteen-room house was built near the original site of Fort Chehalis, inland from the west shore of Grays Harbor. Minnie, as a member of the first Westport City Council, did much to promote the improvement of Westport's streets.

Ben Armstrong was absent much of the time leaving Minnie to care for home and children by herself. Theirs was a stormy relationship which, after twenty-seven years, ended in divorce. Minnie first moved to Ocosta, then to California, and along the way was remarried.

One of the daughters, Eliza, and Captain Hilman Persson, Westport Coast Guard Station Commanding Officer, were married. Son Charles and his family moved to Alaska where Ben joined them. Ben lived there until 1933, passing away at age seventy-six.

After the separation of Minnie and Ben in 1916, the Armstrong house, now vacant, was rented to the family of A. P. Putnam, a conductor on the Aberdeen-Bay City train. Evelyn and Paul Guilford, who owned and operated the Royal Chief razor clam cannery, bought the house in 1923. They lived there until the cannery closed due to the lack of razor clams.

When the Guilfords moved to Port Townsend, sisters named Mrs. Burns and Mrs. Barns bought the building and turned it into a hotel known as the Pines. The hotel operated until one of the sisters died. The surviving sister sold the hotel to Glenn and Clarine Edwards who planned to raise Easter lily bulbs on the surrounding property.

Flower Farming Flourishes

Lilies Of The Fields

Prior to World War II, there were several fields between Markham and Grayland where Croft type lilies were commercially grown for their bulbs. Some growers also raised daffodil and iris bulbs. The area between South Montesano Street and South Forrest Street was known to Westport residents as "Lily Valley." Dee Linder

Minnie Armstrong married Ben Armstrong in 1888. They had seven children. Minnie was a member of the first Westport City Council.

The Armstrong family on the porch of their Westport home. Back row L-R: Elmer Johnson holding baby, Hilman Persson holding baby, Eliza Armstrong Persson, Lovie Armstrong, Charles Armstrong. Middle row L-R: Mary Johnson, Minnie and Ben Armtrong. Front row: Edgar, Lottie and had seven children. Minnie was a member of the first Westport City Council.

Glenacres Inn, formerly the Armstrong home, as it looks today. A wing of rental rooms was added to the right side of the house.

One of the cottages on the Glenacres grounds has its own housekeeping rooms.

planted lilies and daffodils in the valley for a number of years. His original cabin, erected in the early 1900s and a newer home built on the same property in the 1920s, were combined into one house during the late 1950s. The home still stands near the pond Linder dredged out to hold run-off water for irrigation during the drier summer months. A large field north of the "Y" on South Forrest grew both lilies and garlic.

Once World War II was over and Japan no longer our enemy, the Japanese sold their bulbs to the United States far below the price of the local growers. The discovery of ideal growing conditions in the Skagit Valley also contributed to the rapid decline of bulb farms on the South Beach.

Glenacres Inn

When local bulb sales did not materialize, Clarine Edwards turned her house back into a hotel under the name "Glenacres." The hotel ran successfully for many years. Beginning with the upturn in the fishing industry, Glenacres Inn was a popu-

The Croft-type lily grown in Lily Valley was often used as an Easter lily.

lar place to stay. The Edwards enlarged the facilities by building several cottages on the property. In August 1982, the families of U.S. Attorney General Robert Kennedy and his brother in law, Sergeant Shriver, stayed for several days in the largest cottage. The men went fishing while their wives and children visited the shops and beaches of Westport.

Unfortunately, salmon fishing and its numbers of enthusiasts began to decline in the middle 1970s, causing the Edwards to sell Glenacres Inn to Gene and Bette Hoff. Once again the hotel changed hands when it was taken over by Joyce and Jack Jones, Inga and Ken Eades and Roni and James Redman. Major renovations brought the building up to modern standards and it was reopened in April 1985 as a bed and breakfast inn.

Glenn T. Edwards had been a widower for many years when he and Marjorie Kitzinger were married in 1988. They lived in Westport until his health began to fail to the point that he required care in a nursing facility. He died in 1995 at the age of ninety years.

The land between South Forrest and South Montesano Streets was known as Lily Valley due to the bulb farms there. There was also a lucrative market for daffodil and garlic bulbs grown in Westport and Grayland until World War II.

PART VI

Daily Life At The Beach

GAR Park

The Grand Army of the Republic, created for the benefit of veterans who fought for the north in the Civil War, began its organization in 1866. Two years later, the Commander-in-Chief of the G.A.R. introduced Decoration Day as an annual occasion on which graves of servicemen would be decorated to honor the memory of those lost in battle. Now more commonly known as Memorial Day, it is a national holiday honoring the dead of all wars in which the United States has been involved. Families also take advantage of the day to remember those who have passed before them. At one time, the membership in the G.A.R. reached more than four hundred-

The Grand Army of the Republic (G.A.R.) Campground in Westport was a popular picnic and tenting park during the summer months beginning in 1892. Veterans of United States Military Services were entitled to use the facilities.

thousand soldiers, sailors and marines with chapters all over the United States, including Grays Harbor.

One member, William Starr, was the owner of a parcel of land north of Cohassett Beach, south of the Westport Lighthouse. He donated this inland property, 540' x 496', to the G.A.R. in 1892. It was to be used as a campground where annual reunions of veterans could be held for the next five years. Operated by the Pacific Soldiers Reunion Association, servicemen and their families used the park between July 1st and September 1st for many more than the stipulated five years. Some of the members constructed wooden floors for their tents or built small cabins on the park grounds. Campfire gatherings of veterans were opportunities for repeating stories of war experiences led mainly by Civil War veteran, Elijah Wade, a nephew of Patterson Luark and one of the founders of the park.

The Women's Relief Corps, formed as an auxiliary of the G.A.R. in 1883, became owners of the property in 1955 when they received a deed from the Pacific Soldiers Reunion Association. In accepting the deed, the Corps agreed to spend $2,500 for the rehabilitation of the encampment grounds. They also increased the size of the park by purchasing additional land at a tax sale. Although it was never specifically turned into a park open to the public, a portion was set aside for the exclusive use of veterans. Fees were set at $1 a day for camping, fifty cents for picnicking.

Interest in the G.A.R has diminished greatly and there has not been a chapter of the Women's Relief Corps in Grays Harbor for several years. However, two of the Westport lots purchased by the Corps were sold by the nearest chapter which is located in Seattle. The park has fallen into disuse leaving overgrown property on which dilapidated buildings stand. Disposition of the park has been under consideration for some time. Most recently, the City of Westport completed the drilling of two water wells in the park and started working on a master plan for development of ball fields.

Growth Recorded in 1903

The Pacific Soldiers Reunion was an active organization in 1903, according to that year's edition of the Chehalis County Directory. Westport then had a population of one hundred seventy-five persons. There was a Presbyterian Church, three hotels, two general stores and two canneries in town. Edward Overton was proprietor of the Sea Side saloon, John Zumwalt owned the Westport Bar, and Mary and William Smith operated a boarding house. Mrs. C. J. Seiling was proprietor of the Seiling Hotel.

Pioneer Dibkey

William R. Dibkey was fourth Assistant at the United States Lifesaving Station. He had arrived in Westport two years previously from the Canby Lifesaving Station

The Sea Side Hotel had its day early in the century.

Mrs. Smith's Cottage rooms were rented out.

Hotel Aberdeen was larger than most of the hotels in Westport.

A boarding house of unknown ownership has long been gone.

on the Columbia River entrance. As a civilian, Dibkey operated a store in Westport for several years and was postmaster for part of that time. In 1934 he purchased forty acres of tideland in the now eroded Washaway Beach area of North Cove. While farming his acreage, he also carried mail from North Cove to Tokeland and sold milk to a few customers enroute. William Dibkey died in 1966. His son, Robert, lives on and operates a cranberry bog in Grayland.

Babe Bruce Leaves Her Mark

John and Clara Belle Parsons with their five children moved from Elma to Westport in 1910. Johnny Parsons was a violinist who was well known for bringing his musical talents and orchestra to the Harbor. He sometimes played at the Tokeland Hotel, as well as at dances and gatherings around Westport.

Parsons bought a lot on Ocean Avenue on which he built an 18' x 25' wooden platform. As time passed, his tent house became a cabin with an enclosed porch. While Johnny worked at his trade and played music, Clara took care of their five children: Lionel, Ernest, Mabel, Muriel and the youngest, who was named Darthulia in honor of her grandmother. Difficult to pronounce, Darthulia was soon nicknamed "Babe." The nickname has stayed with her all of her life.

John Parsons started to build his home in 1910. The house on Ocean Avenue is currently occupied by his daughter, Babe Parsons Bruce.

Babe, born in Elma in 1904, was six years old when the family moved to Westport. She started first grade in the three-story schoolhouse on North Montesano Street. To reach the school, Babe and her schoolmates had to walk through a pasture, home to a large bull. Though no report was given by anyone being harmed by the animal, the children were cautious and never wore red clothing when crossing the field.

Babe's best friend was Myrtle Wilkins, whose parents owned a store in Westport, and also ran the post office for a time. The girls were well acquainted with the aromatic effects of the whaling station across the water at Bay City, as well as the remnants of whale oil which sometimes coated their favorite swimming hole on Westport's beach.

The Parsons family moved to Seattle during World War I where Babe finished eighth grade and high school. In 1921, at age seventeen, she dropped out of school for a semester and for $15 a week did part-time modeling at the Bon Marché, a Seattle Department store. She and Gordon Bruce were married in 1926 and moved to

Portland where Gordon became manager for the Portland Fish Company. They had one son, Lloyd John Bruce, who resides in Oregon with his family. Though Gordon retired in 1960, nine years were to pass before he and Babe moved to Westport into the house that Johnny built. Gordon died in 1976 but, at this writing, Babe still lives in the house on Ocean Avenue.

When the Westport-South Beach Historical Society was formed in 1985, Mrs. Bruce was one of its charter members. With extensive knowledge of the history of Chehalis Point, Mrs. Bruce has given tours in the Westport Maritime Museum to visitors from all over the world, relating stories about her growing years in Westport. She and her neighbor, Ann Anderson, have spent many hours recording and labeling items donated for exhibits in the museum.

Growth Recorded In 1911

A year after the Parsons family moved to Westport, the 1911 Polk Directory for Grays Harbor reports the town had a population of two hundred. It states that Westport was "located three miles southwest of Ocosta where there was railroad, telegraph and express services. Mail goes daily to Ocosta." There were, at that time, "six hotels in town, three grocery stores, a meat market, one saloon/poolroom, two clam canneries, a real estate office and a transfer company." Nearby Cohassett with daily mail delivery, had one postmaster and one hotel.

Westport Incorporated

The former town of Peterson received its permanent name of "Westport" on November 30, 1891, but did not incorporate until June 26, 1914. Its first mayor was Lloyd Cook who served until 1915. The reins were then taken over for the next six years by William Ingram. C. E. Scarborough was hired as City Clerk at a salary of $7 per month. The city council held its first meeting in the store belonging to E. J. Elliott.

Elliott Families

During the years around World War I, there were several families named Elliott in Westport: Mrs. E. J. Elliott, Mr. and Mrs. Guy M. Elliott, Mrs. Gertrude Elliott and George W. Elliott, one time postmaster. As Post offices were usually located in stores, it is assumed that George and his wife were the Elliotts who operated the store owned by Paul S. Guilford, located on the main corner of town, at Pacific Avenue and Montesano Street. The store was sold in 1919 to Eberhard Nyhus when he and his wife moved to Westport. They had five daughters: Beatrice, Donna, Gudrun, Nancy and Harriet, who was six months old at the time.

The main street of Westport was Pacific Avenue, which led to the first dock on Westport's Shores.

The Vienna Bakery served light meals as well as fresh breads and pastry.

City Hall

During the years before the highway from Aberdeen was completed, passenger buses traveled to and from Aberdeen on the plank road. A garage barn and storage shed was located on Montesano Street between Pacific and Sprague Avenues. When no longer needed as a stop for buses, the building was sold and used for a variety of businesses. For a time it was a pool hall/card room with a barber shop nearby.

Nyhus bought the building which was located across the street from his grocery store/post office. He turned the new property into the Nyhus General Store from which he sold grain and feed. When no longer owned by Nyhus, the building became a notorious bootlegging spot during prohibition years but quickly lost popularity when that law was repealed in 1933.

At a cost of $800, the City of Westport bought the building to house their various efforts. By 1967 the newly remodeled City Hall contained offices for the mayor, the city clerk and public utilities. Included also were council chambers, the Westport Police Station and the Westport Library. A garage for city vehicles was added onto the building in the late 1980s. Westport City Hall was again remodeled in 1996. The Court Clerk's office was moved to the south end of the building, nearer to the police department and the old Clerk's office became headquarters for the mayor.

Westport City Hall building began as a garage/storage shed for early transports. It was used for various businesses before it was purchased by the City of Westport, remodeled and opened in 1967.

Life on Ocean Avenue

Monteith Memories

Because the Lifesaving Station and the Lighthouse were located on Ocean Avenue, that road became a main street leading to the business section of the town. Lots were sold along Ocean Avenue on which small cottages were built by people who lived further inland. These were used as summer homes or were rented out.

One of the new summer residents was the Monteith family of Aberdeen. Maude and George Monteith, Aberdeen store owners, rented one of the houses on Ocean Avenue. There were five children in their family: Berchel, Norris, Enid, Juanita and Fern. Fern Monteith Barton recently wrote an account of their summers at the beach. The following is quoted with her permission:

"Ah, Westport! Memories of the golden carefree years of my childhood and young adulthood are rooted there. It all began when Dr. Berken suggested that the summer of sun and salt air might be helpful for my respiratory problems. What a blessing—not only for me but for my other brothers and sisters.

"I was twelve and the year was 1927. A great part of my next thirteen summers were to be integral in shaping my whole life, as well as that of my children.

"My parents rented a house in Westport. As I remember it, there was only one narrow street called Ocean Avenue. The house is long-gone, as is that of the neighboring large family of McDonalds.

"We were totally free to explore the dunes and beaches, chaperoned by neighbors and family friends. My father owned a grocery store in Aberdeen and once a week would send a grocery truck filled with supplies for his active brood.

"I grew to love the sound of the foghorn and the charm of the lighthouse and wonder how many times we walked that boardwalk to and from the beach.

"Westport, at that time, was really a small fishing village. Years later, it was to be the scene of a disaster which destroyed many boats and the lives of many men. It seems that they were forewarned by the Coast Guard that a massive storm was on its way. Having had a dismal fishing season, most of the fleet decided to chance it. The catastrophe touched almost every family in Westport. Debris from the doomed boats were to be seen washed up on the beaches for years.

"I think we spend two summers at Westport. When I was fourteen, my parents rented the big old Henry house in Grayland from June to September. Here, like Topsy, we 'just grew,' not a care in the world. Many mornings we, our friends and dog, hiked over the dunes and on the hard sand to Westport and the port dock. I remember those wild beach strawberries we picked along the way. Surely there is no sweeter berry in all the world!

"With the Great Depression our lives naturally changed. My father's store was one of the casualties. Rather than miss a summer at the beach, I became a baby-sitter for three little girls at Cohassett, no pay, just my room and board, and every afternoon free. It was just a three-mile walk to Westport and my special friends.

"The Slenes family, Olive, Ethel, Connie and Allen, with their wonderful, generous parents, became my summer afternoon family. On my eighteenth birthday, Olive baked me a surprise birthday cake. On retrospect, it seems that Olive had that beach house filled with happy young people throughout our high school and junior college years. We did all the beach things—clammed, crabbed, sunbathed, square danced at the Ocosta Grange and had a few teenage romances. I have often thought that the Slenes family knew that Olive's time on earth would be brief and encouraged us to have unforgettable fun, for she died during my second year of junior college.

"There was a big log hunting lodge among the pines adjoining what was then Bolam's Auto Park. Junior college groups rented this for many parties and dances.

"One summer I was a park supervisor in South Aberdeen. With the help of the Kiwanis Club we rented the lodge—one week for the girls, and one week for the boys. Most of the children were Croatian and found a new thrill in discovering the joy of vacationing at the beach.

"Later my sister Enid bought that lodge with her first summer check for teaching. I think she paid two hundred fifty dollars for it. It was rustic with a pump and an outdoor 'john.' When the Army of World War II appropriated the lodge for a mess hall, they must have updated the plumbing.

"The people who stand out in memory were the very elderly Scandinavian couple from whom we bought our milk. No matter how late the hour or in what tavern at the dock, when the Bjornsons came through the door, the musicians would strike up a schottische and they would have center stage.

"Important in politics of the town were the Nyhus family. Mrs. Nyhus ran the post office at the time and managed a small restaurant.

"The port dock was more social than commercial. I think there were only one or two fish buyers then."

Harms Family Makes Its Mark

Harms Farm & Store

The Harms family owned a three hundred acre ranch and sawmill in Salkum, Washington, near Puyallup. It was here that their son, Harry, was born in 1895, where he attended school and where he worked during his teenage years. When twenty-two years old, Harry moved to Westport, becoming the owner of a one hundred twenty acre farm on the side of Chehalis Point adjoining the property on which Glenacres stands. He and Della Yana were married and had two children, Gertrude and Leonard. While the children were still small, Della Harms grew so disenchanted with her life in Westport, she packed up her belongings, took her car and drove off, leaving her children with their father to raise.

Harms had a herd of dairy cattle on his acreage. His several farm buildings included a barn, milk house and chicken house. He grew hay on the land stretching towards the east shore of the Harbor. A road that veered off Montesano Street curved to the right and ended at his store. There, Harms offered dairy products and meat.

Harry Harms was born in 1895 and came to Westport in 1917. He had a large farm and the only supermarket in town.

Bertha Ranum was living in Central Park on the outskirts of Aberdeen in 1929 when her husband died from pneumonia while in the hospital. She was now a widow with four young children to raise, no income, and no skills with which to support her family, but she did have an indomitable spirit. She became a representative for the Raleigh Company and traveled around the Harbor selling enough of their products to keep her family fed and clothed.

During her frequent visits to Westport, she became acquainted with Harry Harms. The divorced father and the widow decided to marry. The new Mrs. Harms moved her family into a small house on the farm. Added to the two Harms children were the four Ranums: Robert, Howard, Florence and Maxine. In the summer months, the horses on the farm were put to work by being rented out to tourists. The Harms-Ranum children were all expected to help in various jobs.

Herman Walters, a nephew of Harms, had lost a parent and for a time lived with the family. Occasionally a niece, Magenta, known as Peggy, was a house guest, as was Harry's brother, Claude, who helped on the farm.

Bertha Harms put her merchandising skills to work by adding groceries, dry goods and hardware items to the meat market. She bought a large house in Aberdeen and in the remaining years of her life, traveled between her two homes.

Harms Pavilion

To meet the demands of a growing town, the store in Westport was enlarged and eventually became the Harms Pavilion. It included a skating rink, a dance hall and a lunchroom from which short-order foods were served. A newsstand carried a full line of reading material. Outside, on the edge of the street, was a gas station supplying automobile needs. A large gas station was later built across the street on property owned by Harms. A second floor was added to the store creating an apartment, but for some reason it was seldom used.

Harms Pavilion was developed by Harry and his wife Bertha. The building added a skating rink, dance hall and short-order eatery to the grocery. It was sold in 1956.

They sold the store on Montesano Street in 1956 to Leroy and Peggy Robertson, who operated it as the Westport Supermarket. Ron Christoffer became the owner in 1979. He sold the store to Ted and Marlene Givens in 1986. Ted's Family Grocer became Ted's Red Apple Supermarket in 1989 after the old Harms Pavilion was razed for parking space and the modern new store was built on the south side of the property. Ted Givens operated the store until his death in 1996, and as of this writing, his widow continues to do so.

In 1989 the Harms grocery building was torn down and rebuilt as Ted's Red Apple Supermarket.

Harms Field

With a large family on hand, Bertha and Harry were always interested in the activities of Westport youth. They donated a section of their land to the "youth" of Westport. The property on Montesano Street is today the home of South Beach Little League. It was stipulated in the deed that the land was to become a Little League field and will revert back to the family if this use is ever discontinued.

Although they owned several pieces of rental property in the Aberdeen area, Mr. and Mrs. Harms were civic leaders in Westport for many years. After Bertha and Harry sold the Pavilion, they lived much of the time in Bertha's house in Aberdeen. Harry's health began to fail causing him to be moved to a nursing home. He died in 1978 at age eighty-three. His wife, Bertha, continued to live in her home for another ten years, until her death in 1988. Her daughter, Florence Ranum Hagfors, now lives there.

Developers Dreams

Chehalis Point Developed

At the other side of town, new land at Chehalis Point had been created from the dredging for the Westport Marina by the Port of Grays Harbor. At first, the Port Commissioners leased out this new waterfront to businesses.

A number of individuals took advantage of the opportunity for business development in that area. Among them was motel operator Neddie Rose Farrington. Moving from her original operation, several converted quonset huts known as the Beacon Light Motel at the corner of North Montesano Street and Elizabeth Avenue,

Neddie Rose Farrington opened her Islander Motel in 1963. It was enlarged to include an indoor swimming pool, coffee shop, large dining room and charter office for their fishing boats.

Farrington leased property from the Port at the corner of Westhaven and Revetment Drives in 1962. She bought the little tackle business on the corner called The Bait Box and operated it for a short time, then sold the building (which was then skidded across Westhaven Drive to form the shell of what is now the Pelican Restaurant.) By 1963 Farrington had built The Islander Motel.

That was the same year the Port decided to sell some of its upland property to private individuals or companies. Farrington took advantage of the opportunity. Over the years she added a restaurant, charter boat service and beauty shop. In 1989, members of the community requested that the City Council rename Revetment Drive *Neddie Rose Drive* in honor of this remarkable lady. The Council approved their request.

Development Dreams Unrealized

While Neddie Rose was struggling to keep her Islander Motel afloat in its early years, a group from Seattle, W. S. Piercey Associates, Inc., planned to create a residential and recreational development at Chehalis Point. In 1965, thirty-five acres were purchased and seventy-two acres of empty land in the Westhaven area were leased from the Port of Grays Harbor. There was to be a ten-acre shopping center, a service station, an 18-hole golf course, swimming pool, apartments and condominiums, a motor inn and a restaurant. These expansive plans never materialized.

Westport Expands City Limits

That same year, 408.54 acres were added to the Town of Westport. Within two more years, sections of Westport included Westport Beach, Chehalis, Peterson, Seagrove, Bayview, Grand Army, Golden, Hunley & Hunley, Lighthouse, Westport Acreage, Westhaven, Westhaven First Addition and Westhaven Personal Tracts.

Holand Develops Land & Businesses

Ted and Betty Holand, along with their young son, moved to the South Beach in 1946. Among various business ventures he was involved in, Holand bought the Union Oil Dealership from the Miller family of Grayland in 1955. Three years later he moved it to its present location on Dock Street and Westhaven Drive. In 1984, he sold it to Bill Walsh, who still owns and operates the facility.

Holand also owned large tracts of land between the highway and the beach at the north end of Grayland. Part of the land was developed into three hundred lots for residential use and became Salt Aire Shores. On property he owned in the Cohassett area, he and his partners built the one hundred ten unit Canterbury Inn in 1968. The motel, which includes a heated indoor swimming pool and convention rooms, became a condominium when the units were sold to private individuals. Since 1990, the imposing building on the dunes has been known as the Chateau Westport.

An RV park on Wilson Street was another project belonging to Holand. Opened in 1975, storage units and a machine shop were added to the premises.

Chateau Westport, built as the Canterbury West in 1968, has several conference rooms used for community activities. Thor Lauritzen photo.

Ownership of Holand Center, as it was called, was taken over by Vic Druzianich and Robert Bush in the early 1990s.

There are at least twenty-five more motels, RV parks and campgrounds for visitors to choose from in the Westport area, with several more along SR-105 between Grayland and Tokeland.

Cohassett Reawakens

Post-War Tourism Increases

The 1940s brought their own problems with the War and the recovery from its effects. The 1950s saw an increase in tourism due mainly to salmon fishing, the expansion of Westhaven Cove into a large marina and the opening of new areas for building. The little resort town of Cohassett, south of Westport's city limits, began a revival during this time.

When John Carol Hogan arrived from Wisconsin in 1890, he opened an office in Aberdeen, intending to practice law. Lack of clients during the first two years prompted him to earn a living by working in a mill at night. After becoming established as an attorney, Hogan was, for a time, the publisher of a short-lived local paper, *The Aberdeen Daily Sun*. He developed a section of land on the north side of Grays Harbor, known as Hogan's Corner. He also purchased a large section of Cohassett land on which the Essex Hotel had once stood. There were several cottages on the property, descriptively named "Westwind," "Clam Cottage," and "Blue House." A wooden pathway crossed the sand dunes to the beach. Nearby were stables for horses.

The compound, as well as other cottages in Cohassett, were taken over for housing by the Army during World War II, but the "Barn" was home to Kathryn Hogan, youngest of three daughters of John Hogan. After her mother died when Kathy was eight years old, housekeepers were hired to care for the three girls. When Hogan remarried, Elizabeth (Lizzie) Hogan took over the raising of her step-daughters.

Kathy Hogan married and had two children, divorced their father and married two more times, each ending in divorce. Her father then sent her to live at Cohassett, more or less in exile. While there, Kathy began to write articles about life at Cohassett. In 1940, John Hogan persuaded his friend, Kearny Clark, to publish the columns in the *Gray's Harbor Post*, Clark's weekly newspaper. "The Kitchen Critic" articles were a popular feature for the next ten years. Recently, the daughter of Kearny Clark, Clancy Clark de Nevers, and her friend, Lucy Hart, whose family members were frequent Cohassett cottagers, undertook the task of having Hogan's columns published in book form. *Cohassett Beach Chronicles* is a marvelous account of life at the beach during the World War II years.

After John Hogan died in 1947 at age eighty-four, his widow, Elizabeth, began to sell some of the Cohassett property. Four Aberdeen families were the first purchasers of sites on the upper sand dunes. Ben Weatherwax began construction of his cottage, John Dobrovich was next, Dr. William Hardy then built his house, and he was followed by Ron Johnsone, each, in turn, using his neighbor's electricity while building.

Weatherwax At Cohassett

Ben K. Weatherwax, 1909–1956, was a well-known businessman in Aberdeen who had one of the first cabins on the Cohassett dunes.

Ben Weatherwax, a member of a pioneer Harbor family, had attended school at Washington State College. He and John Forbes, also of Aberdeen, were fraternity brothers of Edward R. Murrow. All were in the communications field with Murrow on the national level. Weatherwax was not only a builder of fine homes but owned and operated an Aberdeen radio station from which he broadcast his commentary on local events. He and Forbes had maintained their friendship with Murrow and when Murrow came to Westport for a salmon fishing trip, Weatherwax and Forbes decided it to be an excellent time to hold a party in Cohassett and introduce Murrow to their friends and neighbors.

The excited friends gathered at the Cohassett Beach home of Ben Weatherwax and awaited the arrival of the world-famous commentator. After considerable delay, Murrow, with his wife and daughter, finally appeared. It was then learned that Murrow had been involved in a long telephone conversation with Dr. Jonas Salk, whose vaccine for poliomyelitis had recently been approved by the Food and Drug Administration for use by the general public. Dr. Salk sought advice from the expert newsman as to the best way to present the idea of a drive to inoculate all school children throughout the country. The advice given that evening to Dr. Salk was carried out and, since the mass inoculation of 1954, polio has been almost entirely eradicated from the United States.

On the evening of November 16, 1956, Weatherwax arrived at his Cohassett Beach home, planning to complete some minor construction work. Asleep in the house next door were John and Margaret Dobrovich. They were awakened about 4:30 a.m. to see their neighbor's house engulfed in flames, by that time unapproachable. Volunteer firemen responded to the alarm but could only prevent the fire from spreading to other houses. After the raging fire was extinguished, the body of Ben Weatherwax, age forty-seven, was found lying across his bed, the victim of smoke inhalation.

The Dobrovich cottage was in the process of being built on the sand dunes of Cohassett in the 1950s. Photo courtesy of Margaret D. Smith.

Margaret and John Dobrovich enjoy time together on the beach. Photo courtesy of Margaret D. Smith.

His pet dog, who had gotten into mischief at home, was being reprimanded and not permitted to accompany Weatherwax to the beach. The tragic outcome of the weekend visit may have been averted had the dog been there to warn its master.

In the following years, two more of the four original houses on the Cohassett Beach dunes fell victims to fire.

John Dobrovich had been an associate of Weatherwax for four years, both being involved in building homes in the Harbor area. Dobrovich had designed and overseen construction of the large cottage on the grounds of Glenacres Inn. After Dobrovich learned he had a heart problem, he and his wife Margaret and their two young children, Mary and John, moved to the quiet surroundings of their Cohassett Beach home. The haunting reminder of the fire that took the life of their neighbor caused them to move back to Aberdeen. Within a year, John Dobrovich suffered a fatal heart attack.

Perry Crothers came to Westport in 1962 as manager of the newly-opened branch of Seattle First National Bank. Needing a place to live, Mr. and Mrs. Crothers rented the beach cottage belonging to Margaret Dobrovich and lived there until they found a house to buy nearby. One day Mrs. Crothers called Margaret and asked her if she was aware that people were digging in the sand in front of her cottage. When asked by the owner what they were doing, the diggers said they had been given a map showing the location of an old hotel (the Essex) that had burned down many years ago. They were looking for artifacts and had found a lovely perfume bottle which they proudly displayed. When told they were encroaching on private property, they left, taking their artifact with them.

Pine Plantings

In 1968 Margaret Dobrovich and neighbor Margaret Hardy acquired from the Weyerhaeuser Tree Farm about three thousand shore pine whips for planting in the dunes to prevent the excessive shifting of sand. Their planting routine consisted of one of the women using a shovel whose blade was inserted into the sand and pulled slightly towards her. The other dropped a tree root into the opening and when the shovel was withdrawn, the earth was resettled by pressure from the shovel's foot. It took only two days to plant all the trees.

It was a successful venture as the pines took hold, grew and are still flourishing, at least those which have not been taken out to make room for new homes. Margaret Dobrovich eventually turned the beach house over to her son, John. She lived in Vancouver for a time, then moved to Tacoma, but missing the ocean beach, she bought a small house on North Forrest and returned to Westport.

Fred Smith Serves As Mayor

Fred Smith, one-time logger, worked in the shipyards of the Harbor during World War I years. Sometime around 1923, he and his wife, Effie, and children moved from Aberdeen to Westport. Charlie Smith, born in 1919, recalls the trip on a fishing boat to the Westport Dock where their belongings were unloaded and then moved by wheelbarrow to their new home.

Smith built a thirty foot trolling boat from which he fished for crab by using thirty ring nets. During that ten-year period, crabs sold for $2 a dozen or 25¢ each.

From 1925 to 1928, Fred served as mayor of Westport and Effie was city clerk. The family consisted of seven children. The oldest was Lorraine followed by Fred, Jr., and the twins, Francis and James. Charlie the youngest son had two little sisters,

Barbara and Betty. When the twins were eleven years old and still living in Westport, Jimmy was tragically killed in an accident while the boys were playing near their home.

The Smiths relocated to Cosmopolis in 1929. As an adult, Francis Smith became involved in the logging business in the Montesano area. He and his wife lived and raised their family there. After his wife's death, Francis became reacquainted with his sister Betty's close friend, Margaret Dobrovich, who was living in Westport. She had been widowed for thirty years when she and Francis were married in 1988. Smith, retired for several years, died in 1993. Margaret D. Smith now lives in Lacey.

The small community of Cohassett which lies about two miles southwest of Westport, has never incorporated nor has it been annexed to the City of Westport. The two neighborhoods blend into each other with their residences crossing an invisible line. Postal addresses for Westport include Cohassett and extend south below the "Y," almost to the northern edge of the cranberry fields of Grayland.

Fred Smith was mayor of Westport during 1924 and 1925. Photo courtesy of Betty Smith Falk.

Effie Smith, one-time Westport City Clerk, holds her twin sons, Francis and James. Photo courtesy of Betty Smith Falk.

PART V

A Community Comes Of Age

The settlers on Chehalis Point began their new lives with the barest of necessities. There was on hand enough food to keep them alive and wood with which to keep them sheltered and warm. The inventions and rapid developments taking place in other parts of the country slowly but surely found their way to outlying communities such as Chehalis Point. These made it possible for later arrivals to stay on the Point, to be comfortable, and to be in touch with the rest of the country.

The Three Rs

Education was a priority with Patterson Luark, influenced no doubt by having a schoolteacher for a father. Before moving from Thurston County to Chehalis Point, his eldest son, Marcellus, had attended Mr. Dillen's High School in Olympia for at least two years, while the younger Luark children took advantage of schooling opportunities available in Thurston County.

Once settled on Chehalis Point, little time was lost before Luark consulted with his neighbors about the need for a school. In November 1858, shortly after the birth of his son, Robert Gray Luark, he and T. J. Carter picked a building site south of the Glenn Peterson claim. With William Medcalf, they built a 16' x 18' log cabin. They raised funds and hired Samuel Jones to teach at $25 a month. On January 3, 1859, the first school in Chehalis County, with seven pupils attending was opened.

In any primitive area, teachers were difficult to find or to keep for any length of time. Early day sessions lasted only as long as a teacher could be induced to stay. But the determined pioneers of Chehalis Point formed a school board and held regular meetings. Board members worked towards a solution to this problem.

One of the original "employers," William Medcalf, temporarily moved his family from their home on the Wynooche River to Chehalis Point during the school session so that his daughter, Elizabeth, could become a pupil. The Medcalfs returned to their home after three months.

The name of Francis McKee Stocking appeared for the first time in Luark's journal in August 1859, and the following month, Luark mentioned the Stocking claim. In December, Stocking, aboard his small sailboat, disappeared while crossing the Harbor. Parties searched for him until he was found by a group of Indians, hanging onto his overturned boat, which was stuck on a sand bar near the mouth of the

Hoquiam River. He had been in the water twenty hours and was quite near death when rescued. His boat was later recovered and returned to him.

Fortunately for the education attempts at Chehalis Point, Stocking survived his ordeal, as a meeting of the school board was held in his home shortly after the accident. The following month the board members decided to build a plank house at the Point and moved the school there.

With the arrival of the Army at Fort Chehalis in 1860 the children of the soldiers also became students at the school. When Eliza Medcalf returned for another session of school, she stayed with the family of one of the Army officers. When the soldiers left Fort Chehalis in 1861, classes were held in one of their vacated buildings.

Luark noted in his journal that on December 31, 1861, his son, Marcellus, returned from Olympia bringing home with him the "annual school fund." In February 1862, Ann Elizabeth James, nineteen-year-old daughter of Samuel and Anna Maria James, and Francis (Frank) Stocking were married at the James Rock home of her parents across the Harbor from Chehalis Point. The young couple moved into the former Westport schoolhouse and lived there for several years.

In October 1862, Stocking was elected school director. The next month Luark moved his family into one of the vacant buildings of the Fort so that his children could attend classes taught by Mrs. Stocking. The Luarks stayed there for five months, then returned to their home.

In March 1865, Emma and Nora Luark rode horseback to the Point, took a boat to Wynooche, and began school classes taught by a Mr. W. Rhodes. They boarded with the family of Joseph Mace, County Commissioner, and returned home when school closed two months later. In October Mr. John Russell from Liverpool, England, was offered and accepted the position of teacher at a salary of $30 a month. At the annual school board meeting in November 1866, Luark was elected school director and Giles Ford was named clerk. School opened on November 12 with Emma and Nora Luark attending. It was soon apparent that Mr. Russell was not fulfilling his duties, as his services were terminated in February 1867.

During this time, Eliza and Frank Stocking had given up their claim at Chehalis Point and moved to a farm in Satsop. Frank died in 1869, leaving Eliza with three small sons to raise. She was married and widowed twice after that. Her son, Harry, died when sixteen years old. The other two sons, George and Fred, both married and had families.

Ocosta Boom & Bust

By 1870 the Petersons were the only non-natives left on Chehalis Point. Though travelers came through, none stayed to make it a home. Five years passed before Charles and Amanda Fry moved onto the Luark farm, but they only remained about a year. Then newcomers started appearing there with intentions of settling down. The beginning of the resort era at the beach and the development of the boom town of Ocosta-by-the-Sea, east of Chehalis Point, had much to do with reviving interest in the ocean side land.

Ocosta-by-the-Sea had its dubious beginnings when the Northern Pacific Railroad agreed to make the potential town its Pacific Ocean terminus in exchange for a half-interest in one thousand acres of land. The survey, which began in 1890, instigated the organization of the Ocosta Land Company. The company's sales promotion resulted in the first day's sales of three hundred lots. The sales boom continued for the next three years. A long wharf was built into the bay for a possible port facility. The town soon had a population of almost five hundred with homes, businesses, a newspaper, a cemetery and a school.

On July 13, 1891, the Board of Directors of Ocosta School District No. 30 signed a contract for an "Agreement for Building by Pepper, Lilly & Co., Architect A. Bradford, for $3,250, total $6,448 a schoolhouse in the town of Ocosta, Chehalis County to be erected and finished on or before the 13th of October, 1891." This contract was to include excavating, carpenter work, plastering, tin work, painting and other works.

R. L. Boyle and P. D. Smith, Directors, notarized by A. S. Mohr, signed an additional provision that "Pepper, Lilly to commence hauling lumber on school block, Aug. 5, 1891. It is hereby agreed by and between the parties that for each day after this date, that the road from Ocean Avenue to Atlantic Avenue remains impassable for lumber wagons, one day shall be added to the time of this contract. Building to be completed by Oct. 13, 1891. If not finished at or before this time, a penalty of $7.50 per day will be charged."

The schoolhouse was finished, classes began and teachers were paid $55 a month for the next eight months. Unfortunately, the Depression of 1893, followed by a railroad strike in 1894, caused Northern Pacific to withdraw its promises for terminals in both Chehalis and Pacific Counties.

There were families still living at Ocosta. By March 22, 1895, four school districts had been organized in the area: No. 54, Westport; No. 14, Markham and Western; No. 43, Markham; and No. 30, Ocosta. When the Ocosta school year ended on June 30, 1901, there were thirty-three male and thirty-seven female children enrolled in the district. Teachers, Jno. (sic) F. Van Dyne and Mollie Jeans, each received $60 a month for their services.

There were several school buildings on Chehalis Point over the years. Classes were held in the three-story wooden Westport School on North Montesano Street, adjacent to a pasture land. The date of its opening has not been determined, but Babe Bruce recalls starting first grade in that building in 1910.

The three-story Westport School opened sometime around 1900. The building, later used as a tavern, burned in 1965.

Beginning in 1926, the one-room Westport School was used for first, second and third grades.

Henry Imes taught in the Westport School for several years.

Henry Imes taught first, second and third grade classes in a one-room wooden building on Spokane Avenue. A wing was added and used as a teacher's cottage for several years. When Paul Hitchcock held the position of superintendent and his wife, Hazel, taught, they lived on the premises.

A wing was added to the school building and was used as a teacher's residence. It is now St. Christopher Church.

In 1915 Districts No. 43, Markham and No. 30, Ocosta were consolidated to form District No. 110. In 1922 Districts No. 110 and No. 14, Markham and Western, became District No. 119, Ocosta-Markham. In 1924 District No. 120 was formed by joining No. 54, Westport and No. 119, Ocosta-Markham. After this consolidation, some of the grades were bussed around the bay to Ocosta.

Betty Marks, long-time resident of Westport, is an example of the typical elementary school student at the time. Her education started in 1929 at the one-room Westport School. She completed first, second and third grades there. Her fourth grade class was held at the Ocosta School, fifth and sixth grades were back in the building on Spokane Avenue. She finished seventh and eighth grades at the Grayland School on State Highway 105, the red building now housing the Pacific Center of the Arts

& Crafts. Though the population of Westport was around three hundred in 1937, there were no classes held there. All students were bussed to Ocosta.

No longer in use, the three-story building on North Montesano Street was sold and the new owner turned it into an inn with a tavern on the first floor and a few rental rooms on the second floor. For a long time the third floor served as a dance hall and/or skating rink. The tavern burned down in 1965 to the point that it had to be gutted. Owner Sy Rubin, rebuilt a one-story tavern on the present site and renamed it Fisherman's Inn, but residents often referred to it as the Schoolhouse Tavern.

When the school building on Spokane Avenue and Broadway Street was no longer used by the School District, it was sold to the Episcopal Church. One wing of the building has, for many years, been the location of the Westport Food Bank. The original school bell is still located in its now enclosed belfry.

The Ocosta School building burned down in 1953 and many student records were destroyed. In order to continue the educational process, other locations, including the small area schools in Grayland and North Cove, were reopened and used until the following year when a new building was completed at its present location on Montesano Street South. The round elementary school building was added to the campus in 1973.

The last School District consolidation began on June 17, 1968, when Ocosta District No. 123 and Tokeland District No. 49 were merged to form Ocosta District No. 172. The name Ocosta was retained at the facilities in Westport.

The newest Ocosta Junior/Senior High School building on South Montesano Street has been in operation since 1987.

Prior to the disastrous school fire, Blanche Pennick held the position of Ocosta School Superintendent. In 1956, L. "Howie" Davidson took over, followed by Erling Olafson in 1960. Robert Hagerud led the District from 1969 until 1973 when Robert Hill became its head. William Gallacher followed Hill in 1980. During his term, voters in Districts No. 172 approved the construction of a new junior/senior high school. The large facility was dedicated on October 18, 1987. Two years later, Ocosta High School Principal, Gerald (Jerry) Jenkins became the District Superintendent. When he left in 1992, Richard Jones filled that position.

Citizen Services

Mail From Home

The long-existing village on the sand dunes inhabited by Indians for hundreds of years became known as "Chehalis Town" or as "Chenamus Town" when Chenamus was chief of the Chehalis Indians between 1857 and 1865. It was also referred to as Chehalis, Point Chehalis, or Chehalis Point. When the first non-natives were getting established, they had no address nor any postal service to and from the new settlement. Letters were delivered to or brought from Olympia or Portland by any obliging traveler who would, as a courtesy, carry mail for the people of Chehalis Point.

In 1859, William Wright, brother of Captain Thomas Wright of the sternwheeler *Enterprise,* was given a government contract to bring mail every other week from Olympia to Chehalis Point. His route consisted of either riding horseback or walking from Olympia to Black River, boarding a canoe to connect with the Chehalis River, floating downstream to Grays Harbor and paddling out to the Point.

When the soldiers of Fort Chehalis arrived in 1860, records show that official correspondence to the Army station was addressed to "Captain M. Maloney, Fourth Infty. Cmdg., Camp Chehalis, Gray's Harbor, Wash Ter."

To the south, letters and freight were carried along the beach between Chehalis Point and North Cove by wagon or stagecoach. Early carriers included Sam Williams, Giles Ford, several members of the Luark family, Sam Benn, Tom Ford and Willie Bergman.

In 1894 George Houk started a stage line, acquired fourteen horses, and got the mail contract. Frank Peterson of Westport hauled not only mail but also passengers and freight by stage or wagon on the sandy edge of the ocean. For eighteen years his schedule was controlled by the tide.

According to United States Postal Archives, Thomas J. Carter was appointed the first postmaster of Chehalis Point on November 19, 1860, nine months after the arrival of the Army troops. He was followed by E. J. Stocking in February 1863. Patterson Luark became postmaster in July 1864. During his term, he noted in his journal on March 21, 1868, that the wife of William Hannigan, who lived on nearby Laidlaw Island, had died leaving four children. The residents of Chehalis Point did what they could to help the family, the youngest in particular, who was an infant. In June Hannigan was given a contract to carry mail each week between Olympia and Shoalwater Bay via Chehalis Point. For this service he was to be paid $2,000 per annum but Hannigan gave up the contract in October,. The route was taken over by

John Gough (Goff), captain and part-owner with Jason Fry of the sternwheeler *Chehalis.*

After the Luarks left Chehalis Point, Dudley S. B. Henry ran the post office, followed by Mrs. Mary Bergman, who served for seven months. Glenn Peterson was appointed to the position on September 20, 1870.

By 1875, Charles Fry was furnishing twice-weekly delivery between Olympia and North Cove. He, too, used a wagon along the beach from North Cove to Chehalis Point, then transferred to an oyster sloop in Grays Harbor which took him to Montesano He finished his route to Olympia either by wagon or horseback, depending on weather conditions. John Van Wormer took over from Fry in 1878 but lost his life while trying to cross the Harbor in his sloop during a storm.

On February 5, 1879, while Glenn Peterson was postmaster, the name Chehalis Point was changed to Peterson Point as a result of the name-change of a small settlement in Lewis County, which was officially designated Chehalis. The town on the Point went by Peterson or Peterson Point for the next twelve years. On November 30, 1891, the developing community was officially renamed Westport.

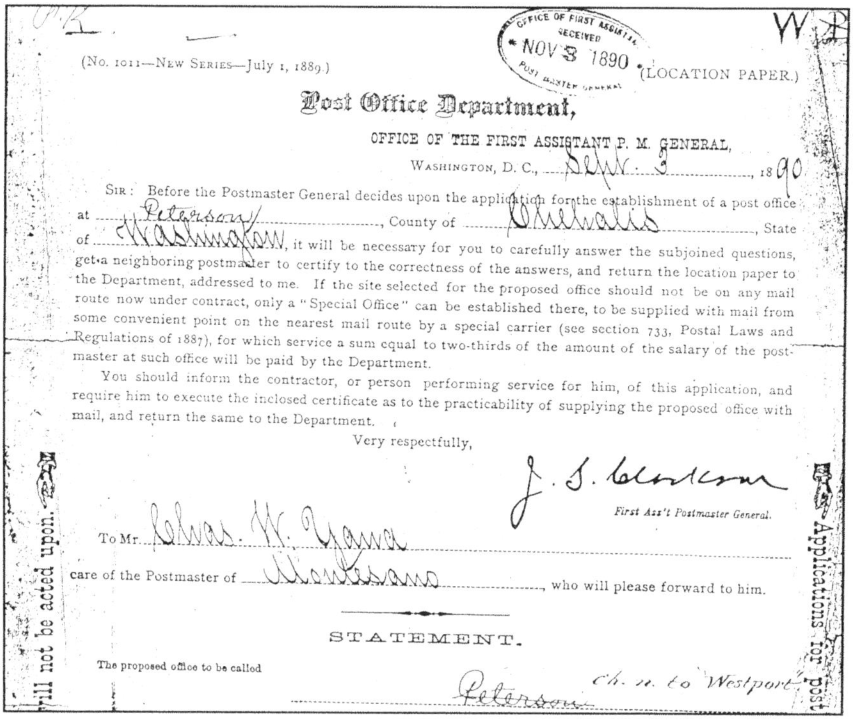

OFFICE OF FIRST ASSISTANT RECEIVED NOV 3 1890 POSTMASTER GENERAL

W

(No. 1011—New Series—July 1, 1889.) (LOCATION PAPER.)

Post Office Department,

OFFICE OF THE FIRST ASSISTANT P. M. GENERAL,

Washington, D. C., Sept. 3, 1890

Sir: Before the Postmaster General decides upon the application for the establishment of a post office at Peterson, County of Chehalis, State of Washington, it will be necessary for you to carefully answer the subjoined questions, get a neighboring postmaster to certify to the correctness of the answers, and return the location paper to the Department, addressed to me. If the site selected for the proposed office should not be on any mail route now under contract, only a "Special Office" can be established there, to be supplied with mail from some convenient point on the nearest mail route by a special carrier (see section 733, Postal Laws and Regulations of 1887), for which service a sum equal to two-thirds of the amount of the salary of the postmaster at such office will be paid by the Department.

You should inform the contractor, or person performing service for him, of this application, and require him to execute the inclosed certificate as to the practicability of supplying the proposed office with mail, and return the same to the Department.

Very respectfully,

J. S. Clarkson

First Ass't Postmaster General.

To Mr. Chas. W. Yana

care of the Postmaster of Montesano, who will please forward to him.

STATEMENT.

The proposed office to be called Peterson Ch. n. to Westport

Will not be acted upon. Applications for post

Post Office Department document of 1890 submitted by Charles Yana requested the settlement's name of Peterson be changed to Westport. The change became official in 1891. Copy furnished by National Archives and Records Administration, Washington, D.C.

In July of 1887, Chehalis Point mail was sent through the Laidlaw Post Office by Alex Laidlaw, Postmaster. The settlement's name was changed to Bay City in October of 1887. On October 20, 1890, a petition to reinstate the Peterson Point

Post Office was signed and filed by Charles W. Yana. Permission was granted and Mr. Yana was appointed postmaster shortly thereafter.

On June 23, 1909, the nearby resort town of Cohassett Beach was given its own post office with H. B. Waldron, proprietor of the Essex Hotel serving as postmaster until June 25, 1916 when it became part of the Westport Post Office.

Small town post offices were most often found in a store or home with the owner or resident appointed as postmaster. During the time when Eberhard Nyhus was postmaster, the office was in the store he bought in 1919 from Paul Guilford, located on the corner of Pacific Avenue and Montesano Street. There it could be found until 1962 when a building was constructed on the east corner of Montesano Street and Washington Avenue. That building originally held not only the post office but also a bakery, the *Twin Harbors Press* and a branch of Seattle First National Bank. In 1979 the post office was enlarged and took over the entire building.

Westport Post Office has been in its present home since 1979.

Mr. and Mrs. Harold Casey and their three children moved from northern Idaho to Westport in 1929. Their daughter, Colleen, began working temporarily at the post office during the time when Mrs. Bonnie Wade Miller was postmaster. Colleen Casey Berger retired in 1989 after many years of service in several capacities.

Gudrun Nyhus Kari, the daughter and sister to two Westport postmasters, often assisted in the post office and was a familiar presence for many years to Westport patrons.

Long Before 911

Because little emphasis was placed on sanitation, infections from injuries were a constant problem for the Chehalis Point settlers. The nearest medical treatment was in Olympia or in South Bend. The distance to services and limited transportation made it necessary for the pioneers to learn to set broken bones, to stem bleeding and to bind wounds. They eliminated toothaches by extraction; the women assisted each other in childbirth. From the Indians, settlers learned which native plants might alleviate ailments such as stomach upsets, rheumatism and infectious diseases; however, they were seldom effective. Hunting accidents and drownings were the leading causes of death, along with fatal wounds from the ever-present knife or ax.

Physicians Set Up Practice

In order to delay the ultimate end of life as long as possible, qualified medical care became very important. The first professional at Chehalis Point was Dr. William Herdman who was listed in the Chehalis County Directory of 1903 as a physician in Westport. Once the highway was opened and it became possible to reach Aberdeen within a reasonable time, residents could avail themselves of medical treatment from several physicians located there.

Dr. Roy Frederickson opened an office at the Point and practiced between 1955 and 1960. Dr. William Daryl Stute moved to Westport in 1963 and opened an office in his living quarters on South Montesano Street, at which time he discovered family connections with the Speakes, the first pioneers to settle on Chehalis Point. Dr. Stute remained in Westport until 1972, then returned to Tacoma. He rented out his office space to Dr. Noel B. Heyrend for about a year. Dr. Stute visits Westport occasionally and while there, stays in his home on South Montesano.

Dr. James Redman and his wife, Veronica, had been living aboard their boat for two years, sailing throughout the islands of the South Pacific. With the impending birth of their first child, they returned to the United States and came to Westport on the recommendation of Dr. David M. H. Lush of South Bend. Dr. Lush, who had a clinic in Grayland, was joined by Dr. Redman in 1977. The Redmans found a small house on the sand dunes, south of Twin Harbors State Park. Their son, Quinn, made his appearance on May 11, 1978, and a daughter, Alexandra, joined the family in 1980. They have lived in their present home since 1980.

Jack Jones persuaded Dr. Lush to move his practice to Westport into new offices he had built in 1976, adjacent to the drug store. Dr. Lush, whose main practice was in the South Bend area, found the distance a disadvantage and sold his Beach Clinic practice to Dr. Redman in September 1979. Since that time, Dr. Redman has served Westport and the surrounding community as a family physician. He is also on the staff of the University of Washington School of Medicine. As of 1994, the Clinic At South Beach has been affiliated with Columbia Capital Medical Center in Olympia.

First Pharmacy

In 1955 pharmacist George Kopsala moved to Westport for the purpose of opening a drug store. Space was available in the building owned by Eberhard Nyhus. Used for many years as a post office and grocery store, the sale of grocery items was discontinued and the business building was restocked with drug store items. Kopsalas' daughter, Joyce, married Jack Jones, also a pharmacist. In the 1970s they built the Twin Harbors Drug Store on North Montesano Street across from the Westport post office.

Dental Services

Dr. Barton M. Miller had a dental office in the Harms Building in the 1960s. After he left, Westport was without dental service until 1992 when Dr. Steven D. Nack opened the South Beach Dental Clinic on South Montesano Street. The former Beach Clinic in Grayland was taken over by dentist, Dr. Richard A. Pedersen, in the early 1980s

The Clinic At South Beach was built in 1976 and holds several medical service offices.

Other Medical Services Offered

Dr. Anne K. Bedford answered a need when she began offering optometry services here in 1990. Physical-therapist Dirk Ralston comes from Aberdeen two days a week. Both are located in the Beach Clinic Building. Doctor of Chiropractic Medicine Kenneth J. Stanton, is available at his office on North Montesano Street, except for one day a week when an audiologist from Beltone Hearing Aids uses the space.

Ambulance Service Begins

Twin Harbor Drug Store was built by Pharmacist Jack Jones in the 1970s.

The nearest hospital and its services has been located in Aberdeen since 1897. To get there from Westport took too much time, especially in an emergency such as a heart attack or accident. This problem was alleviated in the 1950s by a twenty-four hour ambulance service called Westport Superior. As a private company, the little ambulance did on occasion transport individuals to the hospital in Aberdeen, but no doubt the lack of business caused its short stay in Westport. With the ambulance gone, local police officers were sometimes called upon to take emergency cases to the Aberdeen Hospital.

This situation began to change in 1971 when Westport resident Tom Steenson suffered a heart attack. An ambulance from Aberdeen was called, but almost three-quarters of an hour ticked away before its arrival at the Steenson home. Mr. Steenson, who survived his heart attack, was inspired to donate an old Pontiac ambulance to the Westport Lions Club. The vehicle, furnished with scanty equipment, was given to the

City of Westport to be operated through the Police Department, but only after Chief of Police John Regan assured the club members that the ambulance would become a workable asset to the community.

The first ambulance in Westport belonged to a private company in 1956. Photo courtesy of South Beach Ambulance Service.

The second ambulance was donated to the Lions Club by Tom Steenson in 1971 and was operated by the Police Department. Photo courtesy South Beach Ambulance Service.

From its earliest years, Westport had a town marshal to control any problems which might arise from the presence of criminal elements. With the surge in population of the sixties, it became necessary to add a deputy marshal. During the second term of Mayor Bjarne Nilsen, John Regan was persuaded to take on the position of Town Marshal.

Originally from Brooklyn, New York, Regan was a twenty-two year career Marine. When he retired from the Service, he worked for investigative agencies of the United States Navy and for NASA. He was a graduate of the FBI Academy and well-qualified for police work. He and his wife, Mabel, began their new life in Westport in 1968.

Mabel Regan was familiar with the South Beach area. She was born in Oregon, one of six daughters of S. C. and Flora McCollum who had moved to North Cove in 1923. Mabel attended school there until the family settled in Vancouver, Washington. The paths of John and Mabel crossed while both were working in California. They were married in 1966. Three years after accepting the position as Town Marshal, the Westport Police Department was formed in 1971 and John Regan became its first Chief.

That same year, the South Beach Ambulance Corporation, Inc., was formed by Burton Dinius, George Godfrey, Larry Harshberger, John Regan and Mabel Regan. Its first members included Frank Parsons, Jim Watkins, George Jones and John Breitsprecher. Whenever an accident required its services, the ambulance donated by Steenson was dispatched not only within Westport but also to Grayland, North Cove, Tokeland, Ocosta, Markham, or if need be, to part of State Route 105 towards Raymond. Members of the company were Police Department personnel as well as

The third ambulance was a van-type vehicle purchased in 1990. Photo courtesy South Beach Ambulance Service.

The well-equipped ambulance purchased in 1993 stands ready for use in front of the Fire Station where it is garaged when not in use. Photo courtesy South Beach Ambulance Service.

volunteers who attended advanced first aid classes. During the first year of service, the ambulance crew responded to seventy calls.

The following year, police and ambulance service could be reached by dialing 911. In 1973, the Ambulance Company, backed by the City of Westport, purchased its first new van-type vehicle at a cost of $11,000. It was operated around the clock by twenty-two volunteers.

Fighting Fires

In January 1960 the residents of Westport voted to form a fire district. This required the election of three fire commissioners. One of their first duties was to purchase a fire truck. Three years later a second truck was purchased, one that could pump water from the Harbor as well as from Westport's water system. In addition to land-based fire fighting equipment, Coast Guardsmen from Station Grays Harbor responded to emergencies aboard boats equipped with firefighting gear.

The Fire Department equipment was first housed in the garage next to Westport City Hall and, for a short time, in the building by the Old Coast Guard Station. When the present fire station was built on Spokane Street in 1972, equipment and offices were moved there.

As the Ambulance Service had been able to function only with the help of volunteers, it was necessary to find a source of funding for medical supplies and equipment needed in the ambulance. From 1971 to 1995 an annual ball was held. Admission was by donations from the people of the South Beach area. Other financial help was received when the City of Westport began to pay three dollars per member per run, the sum of which went into the equipment fund.

In 1981 the Ambulance Service was moved from the jurisdiction of the Police Department to the Fire Department. Two years later in 1983, Advance Life Support Service was added and a part-time paramedic, Andrew Stubblefield, was hired. With the acquisition of a Medic-I-type ambulance in 1990 with Emergency Medical Service (E.M.S.), an Ambulance District was formed. Darlene Raffleson was hired full-time in 1991. The latest ambulance was purchased in 1993. At the present time, there are three full-time paramedics and three E.M.T.s (Technicians) on call providing twenty-four hour care.

There are four Ambulance Districts from Ocosta to North Cove (which includes Tokeland), all connected with Volunteer Fire Departments. Funding is received through taxation; however, donations for supplies are always appreciated.

The South Beach Ambulance Service now responds to almost nine hundred calls per year.

Burial Grounds Never Found

In November 1859, H. Herndon cut his ankle while working on his claim at the south side of the bay. He was taken to the home of Glenn Peterson but had lost too much blood and died three weeks later. Patterson Luark, Glenn Peterson and T. J. Carter fulfilled a need for the Chehalis Point settlement by choosing a site for a cemetery. Herndon was the first person buried there with prayer led by Luark. The cemetery has never been located.

There have been several grave sites in the area which long since have disappeared. When the settlers were cultivating the land, they sometimes dug up human bones, many of which were of Indians who died from various epidemics or diseases. During the "Big Sick," an epidemic in 1853, there were so many lives lost that bodies were deposited in mass graves. Many of those were found years later while excavating on construction sites.

Some of the local pioneers were buried in the cemetery at Oysterville, and some in the Ocosta Cemetery across the bay after it was established during the heyday of that town. The markers were made of wood and disintegrated over the years. There are no official records of names of those buried there.

There is, however, a copy of an undated petition signed by sixty-six adults of Westport, probably written around 1920. It was headed as follows:

"To the Hon. Mayor and Town Council of Westport, Washington Gentlemen: We the undersigned residents of Westport, Washington, do hereby respectfully petition you to purchase and set aside a site for a Municipal burial ground, and establish it as a Public Cemetery."

Getting Here From There

For centuries the native people in the inland areas of the Chehalis Valley moved about on bodies of water by using their dugout canoes. They created overland trails between the streams and lakes on which to portage their water craft, but the main highway to the Indian village at Chehalis Point was the Chehalis River.

Breaking Trail

When pioneering newcomers arrived on the scene, they took upon themselves the tremendous task of breaking the first trails through the forest from the Wynooche River to Chehalis Point. Led by Patterson Luark on three occasions during 1856 and 1858, these small groups cut a road through the timber along the south shore of Grays Harbor.

The names on the undated list of signers requesting a public cemetery in Westport are of residents living there in the early 1920s. Westport City Hall files.

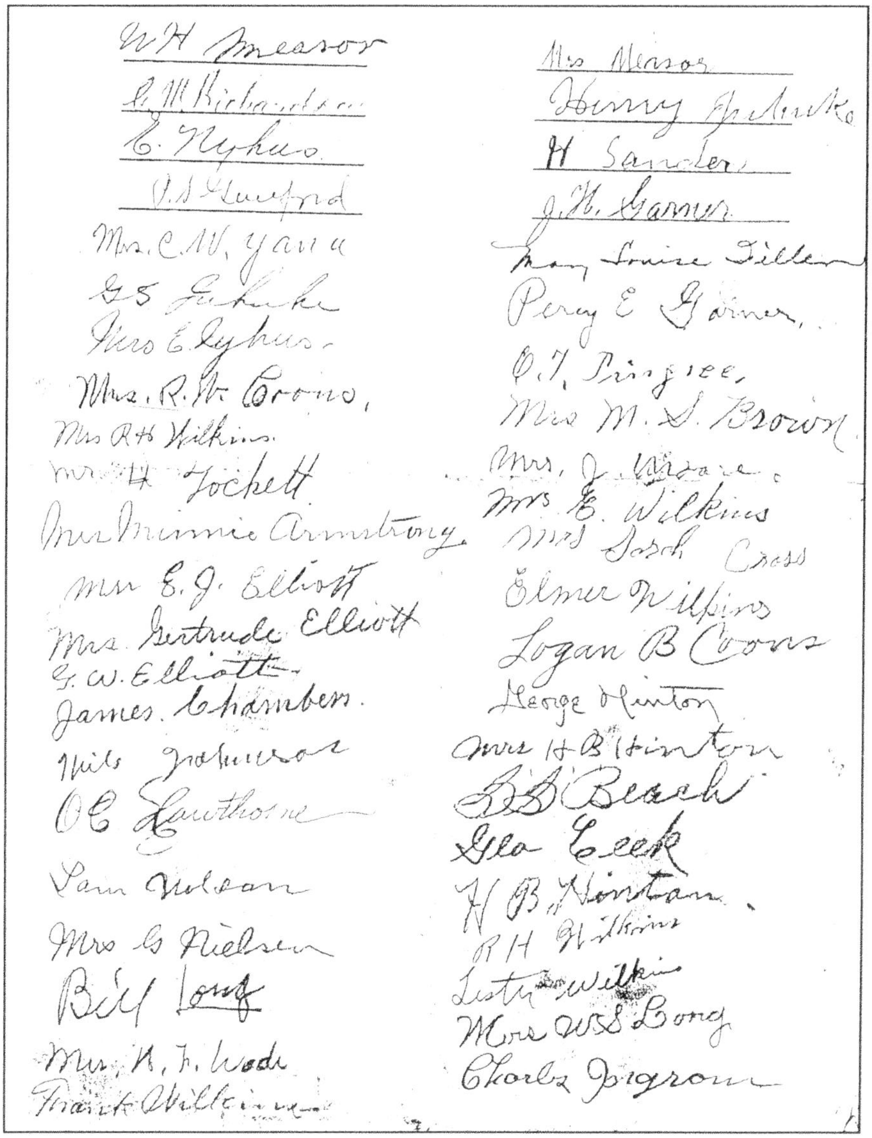

W H Measor
R. M. Richardson
E. Nyhus
O. S. Guiford
Mrs. C. W. Yann
G. S. Gehrke
Mrs E. Nyhus
Mrs. R. W. Coons
Mrs R H Wilkins
Mrs H Tockett
Mrs Minnie Armstrong
Mrs E. J. Elliott
Mrs. Gertrude Elliott
G. W. Elliott
James. Chambers.
Nils Johnson
O C Hawthorne
Sam Nelson
Mrs G Nielsen
Bill Long
Mrs. H. F. Wade
Frank Wilkins

Mrs Measor
Henry Gehrke
H Sander
J. H. Garner
Mary Louise Tiller
Percy E Garner
O. T. Pingree,
Mrs M. S. Brown
Mrs. J. Moore
Mrs E. Wilkins
Mrs Sarah Cross
Elmer Wilkins
Logan B Coons
George Hinton
Mrs H B Hinton
B B Beach
Geo Eeck
H B Hinton
R H Wilkins
Lester Wilkins
Mrs W S Long
Charles Ingram

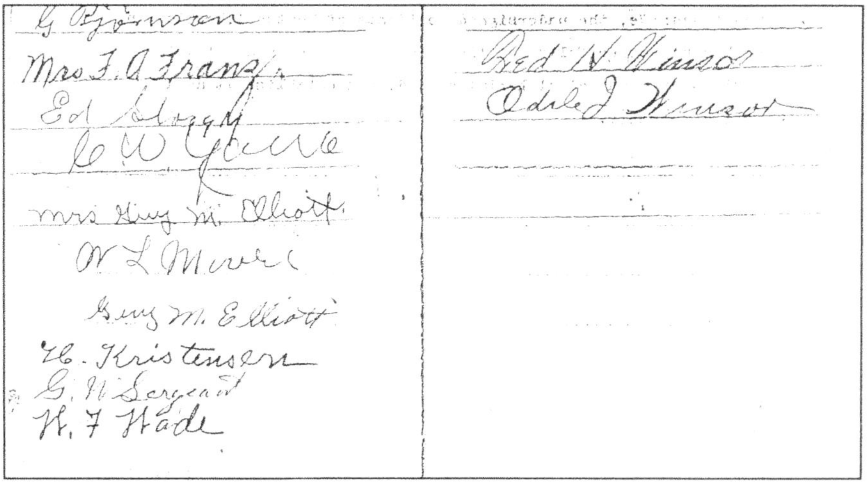

G Bjornson
Mrs F. A. Franz
Ed Slogg
C W Yaw
Mrs Guy M. Elliott
W L Moore
Guy M. Elliott
H. Kristensen
G. N Sergeant
H. F Wade

Fred H. Winsor
Odile J Winsor

In July 1858, Luark, with the help of several of his neighbors, drove his cattle and horses over the trail from the Wynooche River to his claim at the mouth of Johns River and eventually across the bay to Chehalis Point. In time, the land trail became usable for wagons, at least during dry periods.

Ships Sail In

On Grays Harbor, canoes, scows and rafts were seen more and more often, carrying people and supplies from one place to another. Patterson Luark had a sloop, *Bluebird*, on which he sailed the Grays Harbor waters. Early in 1859 the schooner *General Harney* arrived from Portland with a load of cargo for new customers at the Point, probably the first to do so. On its next trip, the *General Harney* brought the family and belongings of Joseph W. McKee to their new home on the Point. Once settled in, McKee opened a general store for the convenience of fellow settlers.

Sternwheelers A Perfect Harbor Fit

After the steam engine had been developed in the eastern United States and found its way to the Northwest, it became popular for use on shallow-draft sternwheelers. These river boats proved to be ideal for the shoals and currents of Grays Harbor. The steamers could run up on the sandy edges of the sloping beaches on which they lowered their gangplanks to unload passengers and freight. The boats' paddles were reversed in order to back off when ready to proceed to the next stop. Operated by wood-fired steam boilers, the supply of fuel seemed endless, judging from the number of trees lining the Harbor.

The arrival of sternwheelers on the Columbia River and in Puget Sound inspired the Territorial Legislature of 1859–1860 to create the Chehalis Steamboat Navigation Company. Once in operation, it was anticipated that the settlements from Chehalis Point to the town of Claquot in Lewis County would be served by steamers on more than one hundred miles of waterways. As a result of this act, the sternwheeler *Enterprise* came to Grays Harbor in 1859, the first to ply its waters.

Over the next few years, people from inland areas rediscovered the ocean beaches around Chehalis Point. To accommodate the ever-increasing boat traffic, a pier was built at the end of Pacific Avenue, then the main street in town. Built on pilings, the pier crossed the tidelands and extended almost five hundred feet into the water where the depth was about sixteen feet at low tide. Vessels of deeper draft than the sternwheelers that ran up on the beaches could now dock at the pier to discharge or pick up passengers. Guests were met at the dock by a horse-drawn carriage and delivered to their hotel.

On weekends, hundreds of passengers were brought by boat to Westport for a day of picnicking, overnight camping, or as paying guests at one of the new hotels. When transportation needs increased, Harbor shipbuilders began their own boat-building factories and were adding their vessels to a growing fleet sailing between Montesano and Chehalis Point ports.

One of the more well-known sternwheelers was the *Montesano*, built in Cosmopolis in 1889 under the direction of Neil Cooney. The hull was one hundred feet long. It was twenty-three feet at its beam, and drew a mere twenty inches maximum. Two engines turned the fourteen-foot wheel. Accommodations included a dining room and five staterooms.

Captain James Whitcomb, a skipper who was familiar with the Harbor, managed to get the *Montesano* stuck on a sand bar and had to wait for the next high tide to set it free. He was never allowed to forget the miscalculation and, from that time on, the sand bar has been known as Whitcomb Flats.

The ninety-eight-foot sternwheeler *Harbor Belle* was launched in Aberdeen in 1902 and was operated by Wilson Brothers Navigation Company. For ten years her schedule was to leave the dock at Aberdeen at 7 a.m. five days a week and travel upriver to Montesano. On Wednesdays and Sundays the *Belle* left Montesano, stopping at Cosmopolis, Aberdeen and Hoquiam before crossing the Harbor to Westport. A sister ship, *Harbor Queen*, and the *Fleetwood* were two other popular sternwheelers that carried passengers and freight to Westport in the same era.

Sternwheeler *Harbor Belle*, built in 1902, sailed to ports on Grays Harbor and regularly stopped at the Pacific Avenue Dock at Westport until 1912.

The arrival of more people brought heavier water traffic. On June 1, 1865, Luark noted in his journal that "two ocean steamers passed southward in sight this week, both in one day." Captain Bloomfield, aboard the *A.J. Wester*, arrived in May 1867 and placed five buoys at the entrance to Grays Harbor, its first channel markers. The following year, Captain Rogers, on the schooner *Fanny*, came to inspect the buoys.

Captain John Gough (Goff), aboard the steamer *Chehalis*, sailed into Grays Harbor in August 1867. He planned to carry freight and passengers around the Harbor and Chehalis River ports but was unable to find enough steady work, so he returned the boat to its home port in Puget Sound. Meanwhile, other sternwheelers continued to make many trips between Harbor ports carrying mail, passengers, freight and sometimes cattle. At Chehalis Point, the boats connected with stage coaches that used the ocean beach for a highway to Shoalwater (Willapa)Bay.

Travelers' Adventures

Travelers who wanted to come to the Harbor were treated to an adventurous experience. For example, A. J. West, who was to build the first sawmill in Aberdeen, brought his family from Michigan in 1884, and a second group the following year. Their trips were typical of the times. After a train ride of about twelve days through the plains of the midwest and mountains of the far west, the passengers arrived in Portland, Oregon. From there, they embarked on one of the small steamers to take them to Astoria, then transferred to another steamer which ferried them across the Columbia River to Ilwaco, Washington Territory. A stagecoach brought them to Oysterville where they were met by another steamer. Its route on Shoalwater Bay ended at North Cove. Between 1889 and 1931, the "Clamshell Railway" took passengers from Ilwaco to Nahcotta.

If Frank Peterson was on hand to load the people and their belongings onto his wagon, he drove them along the ocean beach to his family's farm on Chehalis Point. Depending on the tides, travelers going either way often spent the night in the home of Glenn Peterson overlooking Grays Harbor.

The next day the weary passengers again climbed into the wagon and, with Frank urging the team on, the wagon was pulled into the water until the horses were belly-deep where a small boat waited to take them to a steamer anchored in deeper water. The last leg of the journey ended in Aberdeen, the destination of both groups brought by A. J. West from Michigan.

The *T. J. Potter* was one of the sternwheelers to run between Portland and Astoria and sometimes to Ilwaco where passengers could transfer to coach or railroad.

Riding The Rails

A year before Washington became a state, in 1888, the Northern Pacific Railroad finished laying track which furnished rail transportation from Chicago to Washington Territory. The company then set up a subsidiary, the Tacoma, Olympia & Pacific Railroad, with plans to extend the line to Grays Harbor.

This inspired a group of local businessmen to purchase a large ranch on the south shore of Grays Harbor where Reuben Redman had previously settled. The Harbor men offered Northern Pacific a half interest in the land with the condition that the railroad run a line to the ranch land to become its Pacific Ocean terminus This venture created the boom/bust situation for the area called Ocosta-by-the-Sea. Although the line was actually laid, first to Markham, then to Bay City, Northern Pacific was a victim of the Great Depression of 1893 and the railroad strike of 1894. They withdrew their services causing, in time, the eventual collapse of Ocosta-by-the-Sea.

The Ocosta, Westport, North Cove and Tokeland Railway Motor Company was incorporated in Tacoma on December 15, 1892, with capital stock of $1,000,000. The railroad became part of the Grays Harbor & Puget Sound Railroad and for several years passengers could travel to the whaling station at Bay City and connect with a ferry which would take them to the pier at Chehalis Point. The stern-wheelers which had been providing transportation to Westport were forced to discontinue their runs from Montesano to Aberdeen. For a few more years they operated only between Ocosta and Westport.

Washboard Avenues

Before long, transportation needs were again changing due to the arrival of automobiles in Grays Harbor County. Existing roads were barely adequate and then only during dry periods. When rain fell in quantity, as it is apt to do along the coast, the roads turned into muddy ruts. This problem was alleviated somewhat by building roads using heavy planks cut from the plentiful trees of Washington State. It had been discovered that planks laid end-to-end became a hazard for cars when temperatures dropped below freezing, as the ever-present moisture on wood turned to frost. To keep the cars from sliding off the road, planks were laid crosswise, secured firmly to the base of frames raised about two feet from the ground, and railings were installed on both sides. As plank highways were usually one-way, turnouts were placed every so often. Cars were now able to drive from Aberdeen to Bay City at Elk River and then the ferry service took them to the dock at Chehalis Point.

Wooden highways were constructed for automobiles of Grays Harbor. As they were one-way, turnouts were placed every so often.

In 1912 the Caldwell Brothers signed a contract to construct a road from Aberdeen to the resort town of Cohassett. They had laid the plank road from Ocosta to Bay City, and now they were faced with one of the biggest obstacles, how to cross the mud flats, channels and swamps of South Bay. After careful consideration, county commissioners approved a plan to build a trestle of wood three thousand feet long, spanning Elk River, connecting with a road on Laidlaw Island. The road, completed in 1914, continued along Montesano Street to Chehalis Avenue and across to Cohassett on the ocean side of the Point, thus eliminating the need for ferry service to Westport.

The new road also connected with the street leading into the main part of Westport. Soon after the road was finished, two of the Caldwell brothers, George and Henry, began a stage line for freight and passengers from Westport to Tokeland. A third brother, Byron, became a driver in 1920. He eventually worked for the county maintaining the roads of the South Beach.

Out of necessity, World War II had much to do with improvements to the highway leading to Westport. Soldiers and their equipment were moved to the Westport area as a protection against invasion from the Japanese. When that danger passed, most were sent elsewhere.

In the summer of 1949, Quigg Bros. Construction Company of Hoquiam signed a contract to stockpile road-building materials to be used prior to the surfacing of the road between the Bay City bridge and the Pacific County line in Grayland. In 1956 a new bridge over Elk River replaced the wooden trestle that had been in use since 1914. At the time, the road was designated Highway 13. Later it became State Route 105 with 105A becoming a spur from the "Y" to the end of the road in Westport. Constant upgrading of the highway has resulted in permanent bridges being placed over the rivers and small creeks emptying into the Harbor. State Route 105 was extended to Raymond in 1962, making it possible to reach Highway 101 from Westport, Grayland and Tokeland.

Bus Services

Off-and-on bus service to Westport began after World War II, operated by several different private companies. In 1974 the Grays Harbor Transportation Authority was formed by a vote of County residents. Since that time buses on regularly scheduled routes have carried passengers to and from Westport, connecting with some of the systems beyond Grays Harbor County lines.

Grays Harbor Transit (often using one of its two "trolley" buses on the South Beach) transports passengers from the Marina to the Park-And-Ride lot at the "Y."

Air Field Arrives

On February 8, 1963, the Federal Aviation Administration (FAA) approved plans for the construction of an airfield at Westport on the flatland between the road going to the Docks area and the eastern shore of Chehalis Point. The airport was able to handle small planes during much of the year, but the high tides of winter often flooded the airstrip. A storm drain installed by the Port in 1967 helped somewhat, but Cohassett Creek, angling across the end of the airport, added to the problem.

Improvements were made in 1993 by filling the land with more than one hundred thousand cubic yards of sand, raising the air strip above high tide. The surface was then chip sealed to form a more substantial base for small aircraft.

Lights were installed in 1995, and upon its completion, the airport was officially named the James H. Doolittle Municipal Airport in honor of World War II flying hero, Jimmy Doolittle, who for many years, came to Westport annually to fish for salmon. Doolittle enjoyed his trips to Westport so much that he became a life member of the local V.F.W. Post.

In the fall of 1997, new construction activity began to take place at the airport site. A commercial building with five office/retail spaces was constructed by Westport resident, Patricia Rogers. She also constructed the first hangar next to the airport.

Westport Airfield for small planes was opened in 1963. It was necessary to add height to the runway to keep the high tides of winter from flooding the field. When completed in 1995, the airfield officially became the James H. Doolittle Municipal Airfield. Thor Lauritzen Photo.

Ferry Service Proposed

Across the bay at the northern entrance to Grays Harbor and visible from Westport is the City of Ocean Shores. To reach this resort by automobile involves a drive around the bay through Aberdeen and Hoquiam, a distance of some fifty miles, depending on one's destination. Those fortunate enough to have small water craft could cross the five miles from Westport to Ocean Shores in a half-hour.

According to records kept by Grays Harbor Transportation Authority, foot passenger ferry service began in 1976 when Hal Horton made trips from Westport to Ocean Shores in the *Fleet Fisher II*. The service was taken over by Gary and Fred Peterson during the summer months of 1978 and 1979. *Ed's Girl* and *Lulu Belle*, owned by Ed McFate, were contracted in 1980, and Fred Rodolf took passengers across in 1981. *Ed's Girl* again supplied ferry service from 1982 to 1983, then relocated to Puget Sound.

The ferry *El Matador* takes on foot passengers to cross the Harbor to Ocean Shores on daily runs during the summer months.

When dock facilities proved to be inadequate at Ocean Shores, the ferry crossed to a dock in Hoquiam and Aberdeen beginning in 1984. That year Bill Walsh bought the fuel business located on the corner of Westhaven Drive and Dock Street from Ted Holand. For a number of years, Walsh had operated the charter boat *El Matador* out of Westport. In 1987 he took over the ferry business and began the daily trips to and from Ocean Shores. Since that time, the *El Matador* has crossed the Harbor from May to September six times a day, one-and-a-half hours apart, with up to seventy-four passengers each trip. Bob Thornton is usually at the wheel with Walsh occasionally filling in. This popular excursion averages about ten thousand round-trips during the summer months.

Because of a steady increase of visitors to the Harbor, the possibility of car ferry service between Ocean Shores and Westport is being discussed. This, of course, would require construction of docks capable of loading and unloading vehicles. With the approval from the voters of Grays Harbor County, as well as the State of Washington, this very likely could be an achievable project in the not-too-distant future.

Not All The Big Ones Got Away

By the middle of the 1800s, when canning proved to be safe and profitable, salmon had all but disappeared from California waters due to over fishing. This caused a canning company owned by the Hume family to move their business from the Sacramento River, first to the Columbia River, then to Grays Harbor. A Hume processing plant appeared along the banks of the Wishkah River in the 1880s, thus creating a local industry. Filling the demand for salmon became a viable occupation for Grays Harbor fishermen, including gillnetters who brought their boats and fishing methods from the Columbia River to Westport.

Commercial Craft

The first commercial fishermen gillnetted in Grays Harbor from various types of small open boats between twenty and twenty-four feet in length. They were propelled either by oars or sails. Nets with floats spaced along the top edge were lowered from the stern of the boat forming a curtain in the water. Fish too large to pass through the mesh caught their gills in the openings and were pulled aboard the boat when the net was reeled in.

The Westport Dock was dedicated in 1929. This increased moorage space in the marina, mainly for the fishing fleet.

Double-ended craft similar to those used on the east coast of the United States best suited the needs of the Westporters as these boats could ride the waves easily and could be beached at high tide when not in use. As repairs were needed, the boats, at low tide, lay on their sides, giving the fishermen the opportunity to paint or to scrape algae from the exposed hulls. On high tide, the boats were refloated. They were then turned so the opposite side could be worked on during the next low tide.

When the number of ringnetters, as they were called, reached thirty around the mid-1920s, a small dock for the boats was made available on the east side of Chehalis Point. Still inadequate, in 1929 the Port of Grays Harbor installed a long wharf which stretched six hundred-twenty feet into the cove, adding much more moorage space.

For the dedication of the new Westport Dock, the USS *Eagle #38* came from Aberdeen, tied up to the end of the dock and welcomed visits by the public. The *Eagle*, two hundred feet in length, was one of the numbered patrol boats built by Henry Ford during World War I, to be used to counteract the destruction of American ships by German submarines. There were to be one hundred nineteen of these vessels,

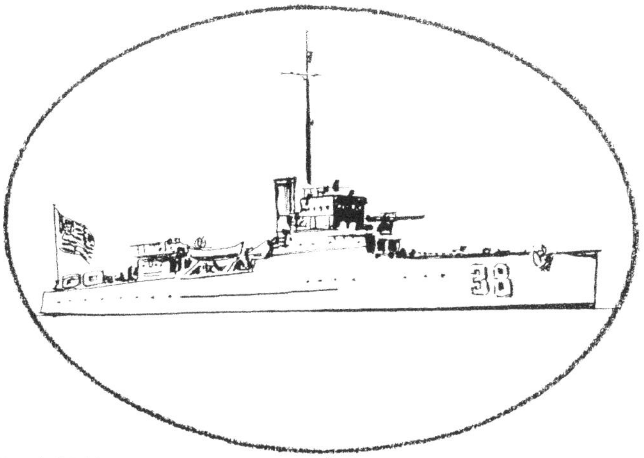

The United States Navy Training Ship *Eagle* tied up at the Westport Dock at its dedication in 1929. The ship was open for tours by the public.

People lined up to get tickets to visit the *USS Eagle* when at the Westport Dock.

but only sixty-one were actually built. They were never used for duty, as the war was over before they were put into service. The boats were either turned over to the Coast Guard Service, were sold, or, in cases like that of the *Eagle,* were used as training ships by the Naval Reserve.

Prior to World War II, the young men who enlisted in the Grays Harbor Naval Reserve Unit were to be sent on active duty to Alaska aboard the U.S.S. *General Ulysses S. Grant.* On their way north, war was declared and the men were returned to be stationed for duty in the Pacific area. After the war, the men who sailed on the *Grant* have held annual reunions, several of which have been in the Westport area.

From Traps To Trollers

One of the first concerns of the new State of Washington in 1889 was the rapid depletion of natural resources. This included salmon, and regulations establishing seasons and quotas went into effect in 1890. The use of fish wheels, fish traps and drag seines were common, but these methods caused much dissension between gillnetters and trap or wheel owners, as traps were far more successful in catching salmon than were the gillnets. In 1935 the use of wheels and traps was abolished.

The fishing boat on the beach is typical of the double-ended troller that began appearing in Westport in the mid-1950s. A cabin built over the engine to protect it from sea water wash and weather gave shelter to the fisherman as well.

By the time the Westport Dock was opened in 1929, gasoline engines were being installed in fishing boats. These changed the boats' appearances by having cabins built over the engines giving protection not only to the equipment but also to the fishermen. In order to compete with fish traps, fishermen were forced to move out on the ocean, but only after outfitting their boats with trolling gear. These boats had masts and poles from which fishing lines were dropped into the water. Weights sank the baitless hooks with shiny spoons attached to attract the salmon. These boats became known as salmon trollers.

As the fishing industry took on a new importance to the people of Westport, more boats arrived on the scene. To compensate for the lack of moorage space, they were tied up to each other by rafting, that is, the first boat was tied to the dock, the second tied to the outer side of the first, the third tied to the second, and so on until four or five boats were lined up side by side. This provided moorage but was a disadvantage to the fishermen on the outer sides, as they had to use the inner boats as a sidewalk, climbing over the railings from deck to deck. They had gear and supplies to carry, sometimes requiring several trips before they were ready to sail. The inner boats, much easier to load, were not able to move out until their way was cleared by the outer boats The situation was not solved until after World War II when the Port of Grays Harbor added more floats, including Float 10, which had fingers.

One of the conveniences used by fishermen during the development of the market was the one-hundred-foot barge owned by Lars Andersen. It was anchored in the cove near the Coast Guard boathouse. Here fishermen brought their newly-caught fish, where they were purchased and sent to other destinations. While at the barge, fishermen could enjoy a meal at the cafe on board. They could have their boats refu-

Nineteen forties aerial view shows the Coast Guard Station and boathouse, a small pier, the Westport Dock with rafted boats and the Lars Andersen barge tied to the outer end. The jetty railroad trestle can be seen in the background.

Aerial view of the Marina before the tip of the Point was developed, shortly after the Coast Guard Station was opened in 1939.

Aerial view taken after the dock on the far left was added.

The Lars Andersen Barge was a welcome stop-over for fishermen. They could buy supplies for their next trip out and could also have meals there.

eled, purchase ice, groceries and other supplies needed for the next trip out. For a long time, Grays Harbor Marine Supply Company furnished the comforts of home to the fishermen when at the barge. A Mr. Remus also bought salmon and other seafood from Westport fishermen during that time.

Mother Nature Strikes Back

As the industry continued to develop, fishermen were learning the ways of the unpredictable sea. On April 5, 1933, with a high barometer, calm waters and clear skies, about two hundred salmon trollers left ports on the Washington coast for a day's catch. By noon, though, an unexpected wind picked up offshore, which became strong enough to cause concerned fishermen to take in their gear. They knew the outgoing tide was to turn at 4 p.m. at which time the boats would be kept from crossing the Grays Harbor bar.

Some of the trollers sailed south to the safety of the Columbia River, some went north to Neah Bay, while forty boats, hoping to ride out the storm, turned back to the ocean beyond the Grays Harbor entrance. At 5 p.m., with the storm at its peak, several of the more inexperienced fishermen attempted to cross the entrance to Westport. They encountered huge waves which played with the boats, lifting them up and tossing them about until they were broken into pieces.

When the storm passed, two Coast Guard lifeboats from Westport brought fuel to boats drifting without power, or towed them in. They found two fishermen adrift in the water and pulled them to safety. Sadly, in that one storm, thirteen Grays Harbor boats were destroyed and nineteen lives were lost, a hard lesson learned by the fishermen.

Nevertheless, deep sea fishing gained momentum and larger vessels with improved gear were built. This enabled boats to travel the greater distances needed to fish for tuna. For a time, sharks were caught for their livers, which were processed for vitamins. World War II caused a lull in the industry, which increased again after its end.

Recreational Fishing Catches On

Dock facilities were doubled by 1950 to handle the growing fleet. With the expansion of moorage space, Westport was becoming the destination for those wishing to catch their own salmon. Also in 1950, a salmon derby, sponsored by Grays Harbor Poggie Club, was held at Westport. Six hundred three contestants entered the derby, and visitors filled the two thousand parking spaces available. The National Governor's Conference was held in Olympia that summer. One of the side trips for members of the conference was a fishing trip out of Westport. Because Governor

Aerial view of a section of the dock area shows the crowded conditions for both boats and cars during the 1960s.

By 1950 the crew of some of the commercial fishing boats were willing to take passengers out for a day's fishing. This practice developed into an on-going charter business.

Thomas Dewey of New York was with the group who came, much favorable publicity resulted from the fishing opportunities at Westport.

Few of the visiting fishermen had their own boats or any of the gear necessary for deep-sea fishing. Some asked and were allowed to go out on the commercial boats, gladly paying their own way, and unintentionally created the beginning of the charter fishing industry. This practice continued until 1955 when four local men began in earnest to establish a charter service. They asked Marine Architect Ed Monk to design a boat model suitable for that purpose, then hired Grandy Boat Works of Seattle to build them. The first four boats were custom-made, forty-two feet in length, with diesel engines. Installed were ship-to-shore radios, depth finders, walk-around decks and dinettes with oil stoves for making coffee. The charter boats, capable of carrying at least ten paying customers per trip, were capable of staying out on the ocean for several hours.

The four boats were ready for the 1956 season. At that time, there were only two restaurants in town from which breakfasts and box lunches could be obtained. Rental poles were available on the boats, but fishermen were required to furnish their own bait. Once charter offices were opened shortly thereafter, they took reservations and had on hand all the necessary supplies for deep sea fishing.

By 1958, there were sixty-seven moorage spaces in Westhaven Cove with more boats arriving every year, and with less wintering over in Puget Sound. Added to the growing fleet of commercial fishing boats were those ready to serve the insatiable market for crab and shrimp. The size of the boats had more than doubled since the days of the first Westport fleet. They were now equipped with radios and the latest safety measures to counteract the unpredictable weather of coastal waters, but tragedy on the ocean was, as yet, never far away.

Lost At Sea

The fifty-eight foot crab boat *Barbara Lee*, skippered by Robert "Bobby" Bolam and two crewmen, Harold Pernula of Westport and Ted Sigurdson of North Cove, was returning to port when it was caught in a violent storm which hit the Washington coast on January 28, 1960. The fifty-two foot Coast Guard Lifeboat *Invincible*, out on patrol duty, attempted to escort the *Barbara Lee* back to port, but nearing the north spit, a huge breaker overturned the lifeboat. As it righted itself, the crew found the windows smashed and engine power gone.

Bobby Bolam, who saw the accident from the *Barbara Lee*, radioed to shore that he was giving the crippled *Invincible* assistance. A five-inch hawser towline was attached to the lifeboat but broke from the strain against churning water. A second hawser, with three hundred feet of line, held fast and was able to tow the *Invincible*. As they were coming towards port, a comber caught the *Barbara Lee* broadside, turned the boat upside down, and swept the three man crew overboard. Pernula was miraculously rescued by the Coast Guardsmen but Bolam, age thirty-eight, and Sigurdson, age twenty-eight, were lost.

The two boats, still tied together drifted across the north spit, accompanied by another Westport lifeboat with a broken oil line. The *Invincible* anchored in safe water, then cut the *Barbara Lee* loose. The survivors stayed in the *Invincible* until they were found by the CG Cutter *McLane*, six miles north of their last known location. The CG Cutter *Yacona* from Astoria, and another lifeboat from Westport, searched in vain for the missing men. The *Barbara Lee* was found beached near the mouth of the Copalis River and was salvaged by its owner, Roy Furfiord.

Memorial To The Missing

The men and officers of the Thirteenth Coast Guard District in Seattle, along with local friends in Westport, collected money enough to have a cenotaph, designed by Bob Kramer, erected on the Point at the end of the Revetment and dedicated to the men of the *Barbara Lee*. Names of other men lost at sea have been added to the Fisherman's Memorial over the years.

The monument is the scene of the yearly Fishermen's Blessing of the Fleet, led by clergymen of local churches and attended by families and friends of Westport fishermen. The ceremony, with the cooperation of Coast Guard personnel from Station Grays Harbor, is usually held on Memorial Day Weekend.

Shipyard Established

By 1961, there were one hundred thirty-eight charter boats sailing out of Westport, one hundred of which were licensed to carry six or more passengers. These, as well as commercial boats, were being built in other areas, not always meeting the needs of Westport fishermen. In 1964, Nancy and Burton Dinius, Ted Holand and the Quigg Brothers of Hoquiam formed the Westport Shipyard, Inc., and began building salmon trollers and crab boats. At first the shipyard could handle hulls up to forty feet; later fiberglass molds made possible the construction of charter vessels up to sixty-three feet. Builders found fiberglass to be stronger, lighter in weight, non-corrosive, fire resistant and less expensive to manufacture than wooden or aluminum frames.

After the Quigg Brothers sold their share, the Westport Shipyard was operated by Dinius and Holand until 1977 when Randy and Rick Rust became owners. The Rust brothers continued to increase the size of molds so that hulls up to one hundred thirty feet could be produced, these mainly for pleasure craft. Westport Shipyard now supplies vessels to California and Florida markets, employing well over one hundred workers.

Westport Marina Grows

In an attempt to keep ahead of the growing fishing industry of the Sixties, the Port of Grays Harbor continued to increase moorage spaces. By 1967 there were six hundred forty-six moorage sites, two hundred thirty on the charter side west of the main dock, three hundred sixty-seven on the commercial side to the east, and the rest reserved for private or Coast Guard vessels. Within a few more seasons, there were almost two hundred fifty boats chartering out of Westport, with commercial boats also increasing in numbers.

Unfortunately, costs of operation steadily grew also. For instance, fuel prices rose high above the original fourteen cents a gallon. The Boldt Decision of 1974, giving the American Indian rights to half of this natural resource, greatly affected commercial, charter and sports fishing out of all coastal ports. Soon many of the moorage spaces, which had been installed by the Port, were now vacant. Fishing seasons were shortened and two fish per day were legal catches for those lucky enough to find them.

In spite of the fishing restrictions, Westport considered itself to be the "Salmon Capital of the World." So did the Lake Michigan port of Waukegan, Illinois. In 1979, a "fishoff" between the two cities determined the title without question belonged to Westport.

The Fisherman's Memorial was built as the result of the loss of the *Barbara Lee* and two of its three-man crew in 1960. Each year on the Sunday before Memorial Day the Blessing of the Fleet ceremony is held here.

Bringing Back The Jacks

While the commercial end of the fishing was increasing, the source of the product was decreasing. In 1978, Twin Harbors Kiwanis Club formed a working partnership with the Humptulips Fish Hatchery to develop rearing pens for raising salmon. Each year tiny freshwater fish, changing to a saltwater environment, have been put into four pens off Float 20 at the Westport Marina. The pens consist of strong fish nets through which ocean water of Grays Harbor temperature is filtered. The fingerlings are carefully deposited into the pens where they are fed once a day at first, then twice a day. The area is gated during feeding time. Members of the Kiwanis group have often spread the feed in the morning, and when the second feeding begins, students from Ocosta High School help out.

The program has been a successful venture, despite some setbacks. In 1995 the pens were visited by five hungry sea lions. With their weight at up to fifteen hundred pounds each, they broke through two of the pens' nets and gorged themselves on the trapped salmon fingerlings. Dan Longmire, the hatchery manager involved in the program since its start, released the rest of the salmon from the waters of Grays Harbor about a month earlier than usual.

Westport Shipyard started building boats for local fishermen around 1965. Under new ownership, the company has expanded into building yachts and ferries for an international market.

Nets can be seen covering the salmon rearing pens. This has been a successful venture except for the one year when they were raided by sea lions.

He hoped that some would escape and find their way out to the ocean where they could stay and grow until they returned two years later, seeking spawning grounds. Longmire respects the ability of sea lions to remember where the pens are and wonders if they will return before the next batch of fish can be released. Everyone concerned expressed regret for the incident, a disappointing setback to a successful experiment in salmon development.

Canneries Flourish

One of the mutual benefits brought to Westport by the charter business was finding the means of preserving the day's catch for lucky fishermen. Salmon could be brought to one of the local canneries which would cut up the fish and pressure can it. Of course, the fish in cans given in exchange for the fisherman's freshly caught salmon would not necessarily have come from the same fish but, no matter, it was all of equal quality, fresh and safely processed.

Canning started around the turn of the century, largely done with razor clams from the nearby ocean beaches. The plentiful clams were worth one cent each to the digger when he brought them to the cannery. There they were cleaned, minced, canned and sold. By 1903 there were two canneries in Westport. One of them, the Ocean Beach Packing Company, was closed for improvement and reopened in 1908. Martin Wingartner, a partner, was business manager.

When clam canneries flourished in Westport early in the century, diggers would bring their razor clams and receive one cent apiece.

Pure Foods Canning Company operated a clam cannery in 1911, believed to be owned by George Scammon, a Westport postmaster. Westport Oyster Company opened a plant in 1913. G. H. Fisheries and Packing Company and Guilford Packing were also processing clams by 1928. Kaakinen Fish Company, owned and operated by Ed and Lila Kaakinen, was open for business at least by 1930. It marketed Sea Haven brand seafood products and was still operating through the boom years of 1950.

Washington Crab Producers came late into being in 1943 when local individuals formed a cooperative company. For many years partner Leif Andersen also served as manager until his retirement in 1993.

Anchor Custom Cannery, Point Adams Packing Company, a subsidiary of the Alaska Packers Association, Inc., Bay Fish Company, King Salmon, Inc., Coley's Seafood, Merino's Seafood, Westport Seafood Exchange and Odyssey Seafood have all had or are currently doing business in Westport. Some handle fresh fish for the retail market, some process canned goods. Across Grays Harbor's South Bay, Brady's Oyster Farm offers a variety of seafoods as well.

Changing Times

In 1994 the Department of Fisheries closed salmon fishing for one year along the Washington coast. Salmon is now listed as endangered due to a variety of reasons. One is the destruction of spawning grounds from logging along rivers emptying into Grays Harbor. Another is the appearance of fishing vessels from other countries in Pacific Coast waters. In spite of regulatory restrictions imposed since 1890, the supply of salmon is being depleted, much to the consternation of those whose livelihood depends on the availability of that resource.

Aerial view of Chehalis Point during the fishing boom of the 1970s shows the number of boats returning to port after several hours out at sea.

Westport has, for some time, been preparing itself for means of survival other than from salmon fishing. Charter boats now take passengers out on the sea for bottom fishing and for whale watching. One of the more surprising diversifications involving charter trips at sea is the increase in bird watching. Under the guidance of the expert Terry Wahl, boatloads of binocular-clad diehards leave Westport early in the morning and spend the day (weather permitting) seeking sight of ocean birds never seen on land, adding their names to life lists.

A young man pulled in a nice salmon while fishing off the dock at Westhaven Marina in 1997.

Westport's commercial fishing fleet has diversified. Shrimp, first discovered about twenty-five miles out from Westport in 1956, are still available Many boats fish for crab during the open season, dropping thousands of pots off our shores and later returning to haul in prized Dungeness crab. Some local boats go north for black cod, some fish for tuna, some go to Alaska for king crab, and some have simply left Grays Harbor. Others have stayed because this is where their homes are.

In God We Trust

Native American Beliefs

The Indians of Chehalis Point held spiritual beliefs that were not well understood by early Christian settlers. The ideas of Christianity as told by some zealous missionaries were unacceptable to many of them. Instead, their lives were governed by centuries old beliefs developed from their close relationship to the natural world.

The Indians had a fear of the dead and would leave a camp where someone had died, never to return unless the departed's spirit was chased away, an ability, for some reason, given only to their white neighbors.

The settlers of Chehalis Point, on the other hand, depended on their Christian faith to help them cope with the harsh life they had chosen. Patterson Luark never seemed to waver from his religious beliefs in spite of the hardships he and his neighbors experienced. In his frequent travels about the Harbor, he always found services to attend on Sundays.

Carrying The Word

One of the first families Luark met when he came to the Chehalis Valley was that of the Reverend Charles Byles. Born in 1807, Byles had received his training from the Cumberland Presbyterian Church in North Carolina. He and his wife, Sarah, their children and his brother, James, joined a wagon train which crossed the rugged Cascade Mountains through Naches Pass, arriving in the Chehalis Valley in 1853. Byles filed a claim in the Grand Mound area where he and Sarah established their home. Later he was part of Luark's trailblazing group, and in 1857, together with the Reverend Jonathan W. Goodell, preached the first Sunday service ever held on the shores of South Bay.

Whenever he came to the Point, Reverend Byles stayed at the Luark home, relaying the message of hope from there or wherever was convenient. In turn, when Luark's business as Justice of the Peace took him to the east side of the county, he was welcomed in the home of Charles Byles.

Another man of the cloth who frequently visited Chehalis Point was the Reverend W. J. Franklin, minister of the Methodist Episcopal Church. He, too, was invited to stay at the home of Patterson Luark when he came to Chehalis Point to preach. Each summer, the Reverend went to Oregon for several weeks to attend church conferences. On February 19, 1862, he conducted the marriage ceremony of Francis W. Stocking and Ann Eliza James. He also presided over the wedding of

Luark's daughter, Ida, to Amos Smith on September 1, 1868, shortly before the Luarks left Chehalis Point.

Due to the drop in population in the years after Fort Chehalis closed and all but the Petersons had moved away, missionaries and circuit riders had little reason to stop at Chehalis Point. Towards the end of the century when transportation by boat and rail was possible, the area began to gain in popularity as a coastal resort town. This created a need for revival of religious leadership and resulted in the first church being established in Westport.

Still standing since 1894 is the first church built in Westport after approval was given by the Presbytery of New York. The building is now privately owned and used for a gear shed.

A church picnic was held circa 1900.

After receiving a loan of $2,500 from the New York Presbytery for a mission project in 1894, a Presbyterian church was built on Tacoma Avenue. A church of the same denomination had been thriving in Aberdeen for several years, but there is no record to show whether that church was affiliated with the new mission, or if the minister, the Reverend M. S. Riddle, came to Westport to give services. However, several ministers of other faiths used the premises as did itinerant preachers when they came to Westport.

The six Caldwell brothers of Wynooche arrived on the Harbor about 1884. Because of their size and strength, they became one of the most well-known families of Grays Harbor They cut brush, farmed, logged and built roads. William was the oldest of the "Big Six," twenty-six years old when the family moved from Ontario, Canada. In 1888 he enrolled at Willamette University, a Methodist school in Oregon, and spent two years studying for the ministry. William returned to Washington State and filed a claim on Black Creek, a tributary of the Wynooche River. He eventually joined the Christian Church after one was established near his home. Preacher Bill, ordained in 1896, served the congregations of small towns, including Westport and Ocosta, for at least twenty years.

According to the 1903–1904 Polk Directory for Chehalis County, both the Reverend William Nye, Methodist, and the Reverend Miles Edney, Baptist, were then living in Westport. It is not known if either preached the Gospel to any of the one hundred seventy-five residents in the town. The Reverend D. H. Nye, a Presbyterian, was listed in Polk's 1913 Directory. Reverend Holmstead appeared in its pages in 1918–1919 and H. M. Bourse in 1921 as Presbyterian clergymen. All were listed as residents of Westport. Information in the directories was not always accurate nor were spellings or occupations. A Reverend Marquis apparently ministered to the Presbyterian congregation during its early years, as he and his wife lived in the cottage next door. The building was later taken over by the Women's Association.

Presbyterians

Around 1920, the family of James Irving came to Grays Harbor. They were friends of the McCausland family, having met at a Presbyterian Church in Quilcene on Hood Canal, where they all lived and where Mr. Irving often conducted services. He was not an ordained minister but was well-versed in Bible teachings, often filling in during the absence of a pastor The Irvings invited the McCausland family to visit them in Westport. Son Bob was five or six years old with little recollection of the trip, but he does remember riding on the train to Bay City where they were met by Mr. Irving. They all got in a wagon, rode to the little fishing village of Westport and saw the Pacific Ocean for the first time. Bob's brother, who was named for Mr. Irving, believes the Irving family later lived in Aberdeen, as he was told that Mr. Irving sometimes rode his bicycle out to Westport when he was to preach on a Sunday morning.

Another Presbyterian Church appeared at South Beach in 1954, this one located next to the Grayland Community Hall. The two churches were served by one minister, Robert Gruell, who led the church service at Westport from 9:30 a.m. to 10:30 am., which was followed by Sunday School. A half hour later, he was at the Grayland Community Church conducting Sunday School, followed by a church service.

The Gruells left the area in 1957 and were succeeded by a retired Methodist minister from Aberdeen, the Reverend Cleland. He took over ministerial duties for about two years until George and Shirley Merrin arrived. They had not been in Westport long before the subject was brought up regarding a merger of the two churches. At first, the congregations met in Westport and in Grayland on alternate months. Eventually, with the encouragement of the Presbytery in Olympia, the governing bodies of the two churches were combined. The Merrins left the church in the hands of Jack Phillips.

The Westport church building was sold to a former mayor of Westport, Bill Wade, in 1970. After both buildings were disposed of, the Presbyterians held morning services in the Episcopal Church, as the priest who traveled from Aberdeen to conduct services there, did not arrive until afternoon. The VFW Youth Center on East Pacific Avenue was used for Sunday School classes during that time.

A dance hall on the dunes just south of Twin Harbors State Park was on the market. It was purchased to become the site for the combined Presbyterian churches in 1971. The members raised what money they could by holding various money-making projects. Extensive renovation was needed before the building could be converted into a church. When completed, the first service was held on Easter Sunday, April 22, 1973, with the Reverend Don Davis leading the congregation.

Bill Wade uses the old church building in Westport as a storage place for his fishing gear. He has made repairs to keep the original mission building standing. The Grayland church building has been an antique store for many years, owned and operated by Cynthia Tuininga.

The Reverend William Ainley began his ministry at the South Beach Presbyterian Church in 1979. When he retired, the Reverend John Akers became its pastor in 1992.

Twin Harbors Presbyterian Church is located on the sand dunes south of Westport city limits. Two churches were combined and began services in 1973.

Episcopalians

On July 24, 1994, the Thirty-fifth Anniversary of the establishment of St. Christopher Episcopal Church was celebrated by its congregation. Services of Holy

Eucharist began at 10 a.m. and were followed by a picnic, music and fellowship influenced by reminiscences of the church's beginnings.

The Episcopal Church in Westport held its first service on July 5, 1959, when a large tent, borrowed from the Diocese of Olympia, was erected on pasture land across the street from the present VFW Hall on East Pacific Avenue. A rental fee of ten dollars a month was paid to owner Dutch John Carstenson. An electric cord plugged into an outlet at a nearby motel provided power to a record player which furnished organ music taped earlier at an Episcopal Church service in Hoquiam. Twenty-nine attendees sat on folding chairs and were observed by curious cows who stopped to look into the tent. Unusual as it was, the church was established and services began with Captain Wesley Janke, an officer of the Episcopal Church Army, leading the congregation.

Captain Wesley F. Janke of the Church Army started the Episcopal Church in Westport in 1954. The old Westport School building was purchased, remodeled and became St. Christopher Church. For many years Janke took time out each September to make taffy to sell at the Western Washington Fair in Puyallup.

Wes Janke grew up in the Northwest, meeting his wife-to-be, Flora in Portland. After their marriage, they became parents of two daughters, Gracie and Mary. Janke was a volunteer fireman and had many occupations over the years, including making and selling taffy each year at a booth during the Western Washington State Fair in Puyallup. One day in 1957, at a Communion Service in Kent, he felt the need to put his life in the Lord's hands and do service for the church. At the suggestion of Bishop Bane of the Diocese of Olympia, he applied for and was accepted for schooling in the Church Army. He and his family left for Michigan and lived there while he received three months of formal training in church history, Bible study and preaching. He was first given a church in Michigan. He was then asked to establish an Episcopal Mission church in Westport. As a Lay Evangelist, he was qualified to conduct worship services, compose and preach his own sermons, visit the sick, hold healing services and officiate at funerals. An ordained priest would, when needed, come from Hoquiam or elsewhere to baptize, conduct marriage services and celebrate Holy Communion.

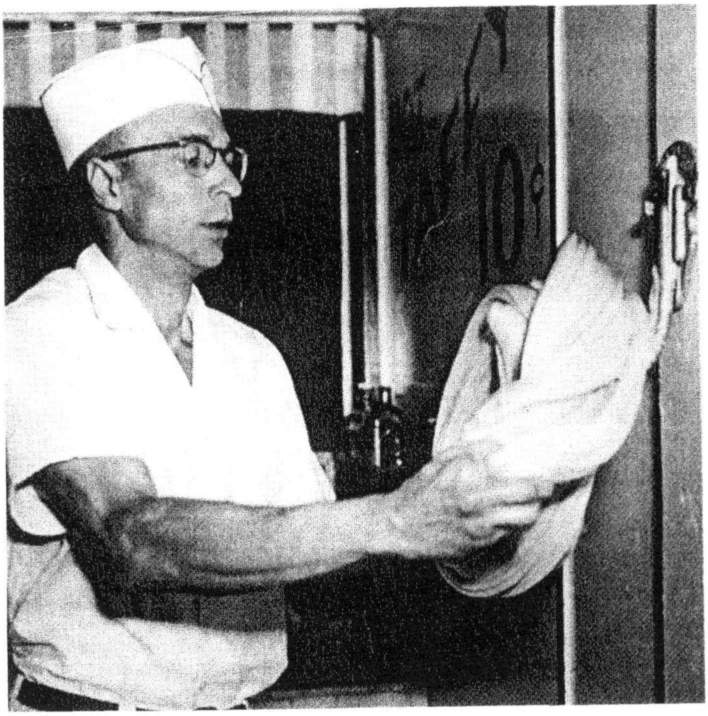

Captain Janke knew that the tent was a temporary shelter for his flock and was pleased to find that not long after his arrival, the two-room school building on the corner of Spokane Avenue and Broadway Street was for sale. With inheritance money, Captain Janke bought the building for $5,000. He was later reimbursed in full by the

Diocese of Olympia. With the approval of the Diocese, an organized mission was established and given the name of St. Christopher's Church in honor of the patron saint of travelers.

Before it became usable, the vacant building required a great amount of labor and materials, all donated by the community. On the center of the roof was a bell tower. Below, a small covered porch led to the doorway. Five windows on each side of the entrance faced Spokane Avenue. One of the rooms became the sanctuary. The three walls of the other room, originally covered with blackboards, were replaced by plywood painted white. One of the two bathrooms was remodeled into a kitchen.

At that time there was much driftwood on the beach. Taking advantage of the supply, one Sunday a successful hunt was held by the members for pieces suitable for the base of the altar and for the railing. A memorable picnic followed the beach combing venture. Brought were four potato salads, buns but no hot dogs and no tableware with which to eat. An enterprising member shaved pieces of driftwood, which proved to be adequate for the occasion.

By fall the church was ready for services and it was time to dismantle and return the tent to the Diocese. Reports on the project indicate that a high wind unexpectedly helped with that task.

St. Christopher Church was remodeled with a sanctuary on the left and the South Beach Food Bank on the right.

The congregation agreed with Captain Janke to make the church building available to organizations for their meetings. There was no charge, but donations were graciously accepted. Five Boy Scouts, Bob Bell, Bill Cutting, Ed Empey, Bert Miller and Bob Putnam earned their God and Country Award after a year's study and regular church attendance. A special service was held with the bishop from Olympia officiating.

Captain Janke remained in Westport for the next three years while the church's membership grew. In 1962 the Janke family took time out, as they did each September, to open their taffy booth at the Fair to supplement their meager income. While there, they made the decision to move to Kent. They later moved to Oregon.

Attendance at St. Christopher Church fell during the next few years after the Jankes left. Some of the members had moved out of the area. Father

Bates of Hoquiam came once a week to hold services, but he was not a member of the community and was out of touch with the Westport-Grayland people. One of the steadfast members who felt that the church needed Captain Janke's leadership prevailed upon him to return. He did, in 1964 as a $1 a year minister. Janke took a job driving bus for the Ocosta School District for an income. Several years later in 1970 the Jankes moved to Orcas Island where the Captain became Fire Chief, qualified because of his many years as a firefighter.

Once again St. Christopher Church was served by visiting priests and by its own lay readers. One member, Diana Wood, a former Nurse Practitioner at the South Beach Clinic, completed studies and was ordained. She has donated her time leading the congregation since 1992.

Many improvements have been made on the former school building. The room which had once been used for living quarters for teachers became the South Beach Food Bank. This program was started by Police Chief John Regan and Church member, the late Marvin (Rusty) Johnston. Laura Hurley has supervised its operation since 1981, assisted by other concerned citizens. Marie Traverso and her volunteers operated St. Christopher Closet, a thrift store containing clothing and miscellaneous household items. The shop moved to the former post office building in Grayland with Ann Anderson in charge. At the present time, plans are being formulated to increase the church size to take care of the growth in attendance there.

Baptists

The first record of a minister of the Baptist faith in the area was in 1903 when the Reverend Miles E. Edney lived in Westport. He may have conducted services in the Presbyterian Church as it was the only house of worship on Chehalis Point. Many years were to pass before Westport's population grew large enough for people to support churches of their own choice. Among these were Pat and Larry Higley who had moved from Walla Walla to Westport in 1971. They attended services at the South Aberdeen Baptist Church where they met other families with a mutual affiliation from the Westport area.

By June of that year, with the assistance of the Reverend Gordon Hyde from Aberdeen, the group began Bible study meetings at the home of the Higleys. In March of the following year, the Baptists realized they needed a building in which to gather. Horace Rowley began a search and found for sale a house surrounded by fourteen lots on South Forrest Street. With the encouragement of the South Aberdeen Baptist Church, whose board agreed to sponsor an extension church, the property was purchased by the Columbia Baptist Conference Board of Trustees. On June 5, 1972, the first meeting was held in the new church to determine what needed to be done before Sunday services could begin. Karen and Roger Brumpton arrived three days later and for two months gave not only practical assistance but also spiritual guidance for starting a Bible school.

The existing house on the property became the church, but only after electrical work was done, a new carpet laid and sixty chairs purchased. A large parking area was graveled. The Baptist Vacation Bible School opened on July 5 and on July 9, 1972, the first Sunday worship service of Twin Harbor Baptist Church was held at 9 a.m. with thirty-two persons attending. Twenty-six were enrolled in Sunday School and, later that day, fifteen took part in evening services.

Twin Harbors Baptist Church on South Forrest Street, affiliated with the General Baptist Conference, opened its doors in 1975.

The next project began on July 4, 1974, when ground was broken for the present church building on South Forrest Street. With help from Baptist churches all over the country, donations allowed the construction to proceed at a rapid pace, on a pay-as-you-go basis. A friend of the church donated work and materials valued at $5,000 for a paved parking lot. The completed building, costing $27,000 had an auditorium capacity of one hundred fifty persons. The first Sunday service was held February 22, 1975. The first full-time pastor was the Reverend Richard Stenholtz. Pastor Dale Hopely now leads the congregation.

Catholics

For many years a Sunday morning visit by Westport residents to the nearest Catholic Church meant a trip to St. Mary's Catholic Church in Aberdeen, or to St. Lawrence Catholic Church in Raymond. St. Mary's Church had associate pastors, one of whom was Father William G. Quick. After he had served all of his life as a priest within the Seattle Diocese, he retired in 1968 from Seahurst on Puget Sound. Father Quick, who had a fondness for fishing, decided to move to Westport for the rest of his life in order to more easily enjoy his favorite pastime.

Settled in Westport, he soon found a congregation without a church. Not one to sit by idly, Father Quick began ministering to the group on Sunday mornings. He first held services in the Harms Building on Montesano Street. When that was no longer available, he moved to what is now the Pacific Center for the Arts & Crafts in Grayland. The Ocosta Grange Hall was next, then the Coho Charters building. With the lack of permanency, Father Quick felt it was time to establish a single site for his fellow Catholics. While using the VFW Youth Center for Sunday Services, he made plans and sought help in carrying them out.

Victor Druzianich at Bayview Lumber Company responded to the need by donating one acre of land next to the lumber yard. Ground was broken on November 1, 1973, by Bill Carriegan, builder. Volunteers did most of the labor but Father Quick used much of his life savings to buy materials for the church building. It was erected at a cost of about $60,000, due to the generosity of the community as well as Father Quick.

The entire project was done without permission from the Diocese of Seattle. However, Father Quick was apparently forgiven, as Archbishop Connolly attended the dedication of St. Paul Catholic Church on March 23, 1974, blessing it's beginnings. The church is a mission of St. Mary's Catholic Church in Aberdeen.

Shortly after its dedication, the Altar Society was formed and officers duly elected. Formerly an all-ladies organization, in recent years, men have been included and the group has continued to fulfill many extra needs for the operation of the church.

Father William G. Quick, retired Catholic priest, moved to Westport and found a congregation without a church. He inspired and bankrolled much of the building of St. Paul Catholic Church which has been open since 1974.

Father Quick lived in his house next door to the church, went fishing and led the Catholics of the South Beach until his health began to fail. He died on June 18, 1986, and was buried in a plot on the church grounds, just a few days before his ninetieth birthday. Father McPhee held services at St. Paul for three and a half years, beginning in 1987, until Father Donald Conger took over. He was followed by the Reverend Stephen Roman, who conducts services not only at St. Paul's but elsewhere on the Harbor as well.

Seventh Day Adventists

For a time in the mid-1930s, there was a Seventh Day Adventist Church in Westport, also a Pentecostal church whose pastor was the Reverend O. W. Nation. Neither church has facilities in Westport at the present time.

Conservative Baptists

The Coastal Community Church had its start several years ago when a group began meeting at the North Cove Grange, and later, in the Commons at Ocosta Junior/Senior High School. They built their own church in "Y." Pastor Dan Lawler had been ministering to the congregation since it opened its doors. He left a void due to his death in May 1995, which was filled by Pastor Mark J. Vissers. When he left, Interim Pastor Newt Rasor conducted services until Pastor Stan Newton came to Westport in the fall of 1997.

Coastal Community Church, affiliated with Northwest Conservative Baptist Association, has been located near the "Y" since 1993.

Latter-Day Saints

The Church of Jesus Christ of Latter-Day Saints, whose President is Andrew Rogers and is located near the Westport "Y." The group recently completed an expansion of its building, which nearly doubled the facility's size.

Church of Jesus Christ of Latter Day Saints joins others churches at the Westport "Y.

Jehovah's Witnesses

The Jehovah's Witnesses, rented a building on Ocean Avenue and South Forrest Street in 1988 for about a year. Volunteers from around the state came together to erect the new Kingdom Hall in less than a week on the corner of Ocean Avenue and Broadway Street.

Assemblies of God

Members of the Assemblies of God gather at the South Beach Christian Center on State Route 105 at the north end of Grayland and Lutherans have worshipped at Twin Harbor Lutheran Church on State Route 105 at the south end of Grayland in Pacific County since 1945.

The Printed Word

Local Newspapers

Over the years several newspapers have kept the residents of the South Beach apprised of local events. The *Westport World* made an appearance in 1892–1893 and was followed by the Westport Star, a publication which set a record for short-term distribution with one issue dated February 26, 1914. The *Ocosta Pioneer*, published during that town's period of hopefulness, survived for five years, dropped out of sight for two years and, after a short comeback in 1898, died with the town.

Norman A. Porter published *The Fisherman* for a short time in 1938–1939, and the *South Beach News Review* gave out local information in the 1950s. *Twin Harbors Press* was published and edited by Tom Trumbull in the 1960s. A retired librarian, Dorothy Bardsley, began a small newsletter-type weekly under the heading, *The Little Scoop*. It was looked forward to by readers from Westport to Tokeland in the 1970s and 1980s. Bardsley was assisted by Edythe Boss, Jean Brooks and Betty Butler at various times until her death from an automobile accident. Betty Butler, long-time reporter for *The Daily World* in Aberdeen, and her photographer husband, George McCleary, published the revised paper, *The Scoop*, until Betty also died from being struck by a vehicle on the highway in front of her Westport home on May 3, 1987. Her husband continued with the paper for a short time.

The *Beach Gazette*, owned and published by Victor Sheets and Sharon Scofield, *The Coast Ave.*, a Tom Decker publication, and the *Pacific Breeze*, published by Steve and Debbie Weddle, all had their turn covering events from Westport to Tokeland from the 1980s to the present time. The *SOUTH BEACH Bulletin*, which began publication in 1993, currently brings weekly news to residents of the South Beach and is published by Barb Aue and Kathie Wahl.

Delivering the Daily

Through all the years of small papers being distributed in the Westport area, *The Daily World* from Aberdeen persevered in its readership to the South Beach, due largely to the reliability of long-time carrier, Allen Slenes.

Cottage built by the Slenes family on Ocean Avenue was sold after World War II.

Emma and Chris Slenes, a longshoreman of Aberdeen, bought a lot next to Johnny Parsons' cottage along Westport's Ocean Avenue. They built a summer home there in 1926. There were four Slenes children: Olive, Allen, Ethel and Constance, whose summer months from then on were filled with childhood adventures found on the beaches around Westport.

One of their playmates was Fern Monteith Barton who recalled her summer days at Westport and her lifelong association with the Slenes family. "I think Allen Slenes should have a book written about him. From his high school days until his recent death, he had to be the Aberdeen's *Daily World* most faithful carrier. He had many successful financial enterprises, but that paper was his first love," she wrote.

Allen Slenes, born in 1915 in Aberdeen, began a lifelong career at age twelve when he became a paper boy for the *Aberdeen Daily World*. He graduated from high school in 1933, got himself a Whippet automobile and took over the paper route to the South Beach, delivering to all customers between Aberdeen and Tokeland. He and Olive Major were married in 1939.

During World War II, Emma and Chris Slenes rented out the house on Ocean Avenue to schoolteachers (They later sold it to a family who was renting it). Also during the war years, Allen was a welder at the shipyard in addition to delivering the papers.

Olive and Allen, parents of three sons, bought a large section of land on the sand dunes south of Twin Harbors State Park. A house on the property became their permanent home. They owned and operated a small store, the Surfside Motel and several rental houses. In failing health, Allen Slenes retired in 1991 after fifty-eight years of bringing newspapers to the South Beach. He died in Olympia in 1992.

Westport Library held an Open House in 1964 when it began serving the public.

Books For The Borrowing

Beginning in the 1930s a bookmobile belonging to the Grays Harbor County Library system visited Westport and other rural districts on a regular basis, except during World War II when it was temporarily discontinued. By the year 1963, the population of Westport had grown to over one thousand persons, a number that swelled considerably during the fishing season. These residents and visitors who felt a lack of a local library began investigating the possibility of adding a public library to the town.

In October when details were worked out with the Grays Harbor Library System, Mayor Bjarne Nilsen introduced the request to the Westport City Council. Permission was granted and temporary quarters were found in the former fire station on Nyhus Street, next to the Coast Guard Station. Josephine Baldwin was its first librarian.

By the end of the year, Mayor Nilsen approached the City Council, stressing the need for a permanent facility. In January 1964 at a special meeting, plans were formulated. It was decided to use that portion of City Hall, which had once been a transportation barn and was no longer needed, for a city library. Aberdeen architect Robert Street was asked to submit specifications to remodel the rooms into a library. He presented the drawings in February, and by March, bids were received from Fogde & Jensen for its construction.

In November of 1964 the Rural Library District of Grays Harbor distributed a letter of invitation to an Open House of the Westport Library, a new member of that District. Support for the library was shared jointly by the City of Westport and from tax funds of Grays Harbor County, an arrangement lasting for the next five years.

In 1969 Westport joined the newly-formed Timberland Regional Library System, supported by and interchangeable with libraries of Thurston, Lewis, Pacific, Mason and Grays Harbor Counties. All property owners in the rural areas of the five counties were assessed for library service through their real estate taxes, but some of the incorporated cities, such as Westport, paid for the service from their own budget, combined with money from the Timberland Library System.

When cities lost much of their government grant assistance in the 1980s, it was no longer possible for Westport to pay that sum from its budgeted income. In order to keep the library afloat, the citizens of Westport were asked to vote in favor of changing their tax system and to join the rural county residents by including the library assessment on their property/real estate tax statement. They agreed by the slim margin of ten votes, and since that time, users in Westport have been able to keep their library open three days a week with funds acquired in this manner. Beginning in January of 1998, the Westport branch has been open four days a week.

Ruth Burden was the Westport Librarian in the early 1970s. Lillian Feneide, who followed her, remained in that position until 1980 when Beverly Westfall took over. During much of the library's growth, Westfall was ably assisted by Kathleen Ringenberg, who succeeded her in 1995 when Westfall moved from the area.

The Friends of the Westport Library is a vital group of South Beach readers who hold meetings with programs for both adults and children. Their goal is the construction of a new, larger library to meet the demands of Westport area's increasing population.

The Comforts of Home

Let There Be Light

It is doubtful whether the settlers of 1858 had any lighting for their homes other than candles or, perhaps, small oil lamps. Once kerosene became popular, lamps using this fuel were found in most of the houses in Westport. Some of the more fortunate families had on their premises carbide light plants made possible by a gas-producing chemical, commonly found in rural areas before electrical power lines reached the outlying districts.

The development of electrical power had a momentous impact on the entire world. New light forms cropped up rapidly in cities of concentrated population, but they were long in coming to areas such as Chehalis Point. By the 1920s, small independent plants were showing up around Grays Harbor, including Cohasset Power and Light Company on the South Beach. Residents of Grays Harbor County voted in 1938 to form a unified electric power company. The Public Utility District (PUD) No. 1 of Grays Harbor was incorporated in 1940 under the control of three commissioners, but expansion to some of the rural areas was halted until after the end of World War II. The PUD then bought out the Twin Harbors Electric Company and its lines south to Toke Point.

Electric Park in Aberdeen, originally owned by Grays Harbor Railway and Light Company, became the home of the steam-operated sawdust-burning electric plant from which electricity flowed all over the county, not only to Westport but to Tokeland in Pacific County. Along with the growth in population, the use of electricity increased, creating the constant need for new equipment and expansion of its services.

Residents of the South Beach area were soon able to take their electrical services for granted, sorely missed when one of the violent winds swept in from the ocean leaving broken power lines caused by falling trees. When power is cut off, lines are repaired as quickly as possible by efficient linesmen who must often work while storms are raging, the very conditions which brought about the outage. This happens less frequently now that the land edging the highway and streets is kept clear of tall native growths, away from the power lines.

Number, Please

Cohassett Beach Telephone Company, established in 1911 by J. B. Benson, provided service from Aberdeen through Bay City to Cohassett Beach and in 1915 was given permission to install lines in Westport.

Three years later William C. and Myrtle Mumaw, former managers of Pacific Telephone and Telegraph Company in Aberdeen, began to operate the system.

Ownership of the company was taken over in 1940 by their son and daughter-in-law, R. Henry and Bethel Mumaw. By this time, lines had been extended throughout the Westport area and south to Tokeland.

A large section of land north of the Westport "Y" belonging to I. A. McDonald, Harold Lillegaard and the Women's Association of the Presbyterian Church, was purchased by the Mumaws in 1953. Their office was built on that property along State Route 105.

Cohassett Telephone began a two-year underground wiring program in 1965 with other modernization plans also under consideration. As telephone technology was advancing faster than the company could absorb it, the Mumaws decided in 1967 to sell out to Continental Telephone Corporation. Continental was a large independent company which had facilities and the financial means to keep abreast with the accelerated developments of the communications industry. George Godfrey, a telephone technician with Continental, was transferred to Westport to assist the Mumaws, who had agreed to manage the system during its transition period.

When the Cohassett Company name was officially changed to Continental Telephone in 1972, the Mumaws retired to their new home near the "Y," later purchased by Sharon and Cliff Beatty. Continental sold the former South Beach system to General Telephone and Electric (GTE) in 1991.

Changing Channels

After World War II television became a popular form of entertainment for the residents of Westport. Antennas began to appear on the skyline in an attempt to improve the almost non-existent images being received on their screens. The best solution was to connect television sets to a cable system, companies of which were forming in many areas. This prompted Julius Furford of Grayland, inventor of the Furford Picker used by cranberry growers, and Ted Holand, who had experience in the television industry, to form the Grayland Television Cable Company.

Incorporated in 1958, it joined several other small companies in the Harbor area. The consolidation enabled a much better picture to be transmitted by microwave from Capitol Peak near Olympia to the top of the Finch Building in Aberdeen.

The Grayland Cable Company operated until 1976 when Fred Goddard of Aberdeen and others bought out the co-owners. For several years Harbor Videocable was the owner; then it changed hands to Cooke Cablevision, Inc. In 1987 it became Cablevision of Washington, Inc., but since 1990 the company has been a part of the giant Telecommunications, Inc., known as TCI.

Cool, Clear, Water

As early residents moved onto the Point, they first dug wells on their properties for a supply of fresh water. By the end of the century, a water system for the town was created. Water from four wells was pumped into a 125,000 gallon elevated steel tank, connected by lines to homes and businesses. Located south of the City Park, the tank was visible from the ocean and used as a landmark by passing vessels for many years.

When that tank's capacity became inadequate, a 12.4 million gallon reservoir was erected. There are now two huge standpipe tanks furnishing water. One of the Rusty Buckets, as they are called, due to their shape and color, rises from the ground on South Montesano Street, the other near the old elevated tank which was recently removed.

Royal Flush

Sewage disposal, always a problem for concentrated population areas, was alleviated in 1976 when the United States Government gave Westport a grant through HUD for the construction of a sewer plant. Up until that time, Westport residents made do with cesspools, French Drains and septic tanks. The new system allows water from the treatment plant to filter through the sandy soil of its drainage field before it is discharged into the bay on the east side of the peninsula. Processed and sterilized solid waste has been salvaged and is available to the public for use as fertilizer. Located near Half Moon Bay, erosion of the nearby ocean front has caused some concern as to its stability, but the U.S. Army Corps of Engineers has done extensive work to alleviate the problem. It is currently being reconstructed.

When water and sewer lines were originally installed in Westport's streets, no maps were made of their location which has created an ongoing problem for future development.

Promoting Commerce

Check, Please

Seattle First National Bank opened a branch in Westport in 1962 with Perry Crothers as its manager. The bank's office was first located in the building on North Montesano Street, sharing space with the local post office. When space became inad-

Seattle First National Bank, known as SeaFirst, came to Westport in 1962 and moved to its present building in 1979.

equate, a new larger office building was opened in October 1979 a short distance away where it is still located today.

Aberdeen Federal Savings and Loan moved a mobile unit to Westport in 1972. Its successful operation instigated the construction of a new building, also on North Montesano Street four years later. In 1990 the parent office in Aberdeen changed its name to Anchor Savings Bank due to expanding business in Southwest Washington. Plans are now in the works for a new Anchor Savings building, still on North

Aberdeen Federal Savings and Loan opened an office in Westport in 1972 and moved into its present quarters in 1976. The company changed its name to Anchor Savings Bank in 1990. A new building will be constructed soon across the street and one block north.

Montesano Street but a couple of blocks north on the opposite side. The target date for its opening was the spring of 1998.

Twin Harbors Beach Resort Association

The first organization to promote business enterprises on the South Beach became a reality in 1948 when Clarine Edwards of the Glenacres Motel and Mrs. Vern Mason of the Gables, both in Westport, started the Twin Harbors Beach Resort Association that year. The main purpose was to publish a brochure, to get to know each other in the trade better, and to see each other's cabins and motels along the entire beach. The latter was taken care of by an annual spring caravan to each business.

Active members were owners and operators of motels and resorts from Westport to Tokeland. Other business owners were allowed to become Associate members with no voting privileges.

The organization was active in promoting tourism, in getting the highway from the South Beach area to Raymond, in obtaining highway signs promoting the area, in upgrading businesses, always keeping in mind the main purpose of making the visitor happy with the area.

In 1962 when the World's Fair in Seattle increased the emphasis on tourism throughout Washington state, the group opened an Information Center. In 1963 The Twin Harbors Beach Resort Association changed its name to the Twin Harbors

Beach Association with membership open to all businesses. Associate memberships were eliminated at that time. In the summer of 1993 the Association became the umbrella organization for the formation of the Cranberry Coast Chamber of Commerce, the third such business owner's organization on the South Beach.

Pacific Highway Association

The Pacific Highway Association was formed in 1962 and the Association was most active in these meetings under the leadership of seafood canner and seller, Ward Coley, with Orville Engle and Harold Peterson serving as committee members.

Clam Conservation Committee

In 1962–1964 there was formed for the first time a three beach, North Cove, Long Beach and Twin Harbors, Clam Conservation Committee with Harold Peterson as its Chairman. The group at this time also sponsored the prohibition of beach driving one hour after sunset and one hour before sunrise on a year around basis. More highway signs were developed and placed around Grays Harbor, Pacific and Lewis counties.

Westport/Grayland Chamber

On March 26, 1953, the Secretary of State of Washington approved Articles of Incorporation for the Westport Chamber of Commerce: "The objects and purposes for which this corporation is formed and the powers thereof are and shall be to promote the civic, commercial and industrial welfare of Westport."

There were seven original Directors of the Board: William Wade, H. L. Dotson, Don Marlow, R. P. Boohm, Henry Mumaw, Mabel Hart and Harry Harms. The organization was renamed The Westport-Grayland Chamber of Commerce when a number of Grayland businesses joined the organization.

The Westport-Grayland Chamber of Commerce is a sponsor of many local activities, such as gray whale watching with weekend educational seminars, the Annual Crab Races and Crab Feed, the Blessing of the Fleet ceremony, the Seafood Festival, Craft Shows, etc. The year ends with a Holiday Social and Silent Auction for the community. The group also brings in Santa-by-the-Sea to entertain children and holds a Holiday Home and Business Decorating Contest with prizes to encourage Christmas decorations.

The Chamber's offices have been in several locations in Westport. For a time it was in the Old Coast Guard Station. A small building on North Montesano Street near the airport was its home for several years until offices were set up in a building at the Westport "Y" that houses a Grays Harbor Public Utility District pay station and a former real estate office.

After leasing the building for several years, in 1996 the Chamber bought the building and adjacent property for parking from Grays Harbor PUD.

Other Chambers Form

Two other Chambers have also formed on the South Beach in recent years. Desiring more control over promotion of their specific areas, business owners in Tokeland formed the Tokeland Chamber of Commerce in 1986. In 1993 members of Twin Harbors Beach Association voted to become a full-fledged Chamber of Commerce, calling themselves the Cranberry Coast Chamber of Commerce in an effort to promote more strongly businesses outside of the Westport City limits.

While the Westport Chamber has the most members, some businesses have opted to join two or even all three of the organizations.

Time Out For Play

State Parks Come To The Beach

The State Board of Park Commissioners, forerunner of the Washington State Parks and Recreation Commission, had its start in 1913. Several years later, there were

A road in Twin Harbors State Park has campsites on each side.

eleven state parks and seven small parcels of particular interest or scenic beauty that had been designated for public use. By 1935 the Washington State system had twenty-one parks under its jurisdiction, but as yet no land had been set aside along the Pacific Ocean shoreline. To remedy this omission, a United States Training Ground south of Cohassett Beach, no longer in use, was acquired by the Parks Commission. Army barracks existing on the land were useful for a time but were gradually taken out, the last being removed in 1977. From March 1939 to March 1991, fifteen parcels of land were combined to form Twin Harbors State Park. The area now consists of one hundred seventy-two acres with 3,414 feet of ocean shoreline.

The Twin Harbors State Park Ranger also has under his supervision Westhaven State Park, almost eighty acres depending on the amount of erosion occurring at Chehalis Point. This is land formerly belonging to the Port of Grays Harbor, accreted after the construction of the South Jetty and includes dredging spoils from out of Grays Harbor. On June 24, 1968, the State of Washington was given a deed, free of charge, by the Port of Grays Harbor for this land.

Erosion Threat

Serious erosion began in 1988 when winter storms washed out the land on which the building housing the public restrooms and showers and part of the parking lot were located. Further erosion in 1995 forced the Parks Service to dismantle and remove a second restroom facility threatened by continued erosion. In December of

Erosion at Westhaven State Park washed away the parking lot in 1993 and then created a breach along the South Jetty between the ocean and Half Moon Bay in December of 1994. A temporary fix had the U.S. Army Corps of Engineers filling the area with sand, with an extension of the South Jetty all the way across Half Moon Bay in the works. The *Daily World* photo.

the same year a breach occurred between the South Jetty and Half Moon Bay to the east. The City of Westport declared a State of Emergency, and federal funding was secured to provide 270,000 cubic yards of sand fill to close the gap.

Allowing the breach to remain would have not only destroyed the city's wastewater treatment facility, but would have allowed the ocean to overrun the City's vital Docks area business and residential community. At risk, also, was the South Jetty, vital to keeping the Grays Harbor Channel shipping lane open.

The U.S. Army Corps of Engineers ran a pipeline from Firecracker Point near the U.S. Coast Guard Station across the entire width of Point Chehalis to Half Moon Bay. The line carried dredge spoils from the Harbor, combined with an easily pumped slurry.

Over a period of three months, in the spring and summer of 1996, the added sand reclaimed the State Park land, reconnecting it with the South Jetty.

Admittedly a stop-gap measure, plans are now in the works for an extension east of the jetty and an extension westward of the revetment along Half Moon Bay's eastern shore until the two join. Work was expected to begin on this project in the summer of 1998.

The ocean waves next to the jetty bring surfers year round to Westhaven State Park.

The ocean waves coming to shore on the south side of the jetty have resulted in a popular surf boarding area, challenging enough to bring surfers from many parts of the world to participate in annual contests.

Beach By-way A Highway

Because of the need for access to the razor clam beds and for beach combing between Westport and Tokeland, vehicular traffic has been allowed on the beach, subject to the same laws applying to state highways. The driver must be licensed as well as his vehicle and must abide by the speed limit of twenty-five miles per hour, keeping in mind that pedestrians always have the right-of-way.

In 1988 the Washington State Legislature amended the traffic laws of the shoreline. There are areas along the beach where no driving is allowed, such as in front of Westhaven State Park between the South Jetty and the Grays Harbor Lighthouse, as well as south of the Warrenton Cannery Road Beach access. Driving is not allowed on some other areas of the beach between April 15 and Labor Day. On those portions of the beach where driving is allowed, the State Highway Rules of the Road apply.

DuneTrail A Trekker's Treat

Lack of access to the beach on State Park property prevented many from enjoying the scenery along the ocean from Westport to North Cove. To compensate for the ban on beach driving, a plan was formed to create a trail along the dunes overlooking the ocean. Supported by Westport Mayor Harold Hardy, the Westport City Council and Washington State Parks, the plan was set in motion. To cover the approximate cost of $204,000, grants were sought and received from the Washington State Parks Department and the Department of Natural Resources. The City of Westport con-

The Westport Lighthouse DuneTrail is just over a mile long. The eight-foot wide cement walkway is a popular place for walking as it winds through the sand dunes between Westhaven State Park and Westport Light State Park.

Looking west from the trail is the Pacific Ocean, to the east can be seen the Westport Lighthouse as it rises above the trees.

tributed $1,000 to cover the balance. The untimely death of Mayor Hardy in 1990 did not delay the project.

The Trail, edged in beach grasses and wildflowers, was opened in 1993. Nearly six thousand feet long and eight feet wide, the Westport Lighthouse Trail was paved for use by disabled persons and for bicycles. There are three platforms overlooking the ocean, and better than a dozen memorial benches donated by private citizens and businesses that are conveniently located along its length. The Beach Trail winds through the sand dunes between the parking lots of Westhaven State Park and Westport Light State Park. Regardless of weather, people use the trail for daytime walks, sometimes going the entire distance and returning, sometimes walking part way and returning, or having someone drop walkers off with a designated driver going from one parking area to the other to meet them at trek's end.

Westport Light State Park

Westport Light State Park is a recreation area with almost three thousand four hundred feet of ocean frontage, and consists of over two hundred twelve acres. Two more parcels were acquired from the United States Government at a cost of $29,000, one in 1971 and the other in 1975. There are no camping facilities around the large parking lot, but the park is an excellent place to picnic, to fly kites and to play on the beach during daylight hours. The first order Fresnel lens in the Grays Harbor Light nearby is no longer in service. It was replaced in 1987 with a beacon attached to its front rail. Generally closed to the public, the lighthouse is sometimes open to visitors on holiday weekends by arrangement with the U.S. Coast Guard. Tours are provided by members of the local historical society.

Grayland State Park

Grayland State Park, part of the Twin Harbors system, is just south of the Grays Harbor County line. The land was acquired between 1959 and 1981 in twelve separate parcels. It includes almost seven thousand five hundred feet of ocean frontage and its four hundred one acres have ample room for sixty trailer sites in its campground.

All the shoreline from Chehalis Point to the entrance of Willapa Bay belong to the State of Washington Parks and Recreation Commission. The edge, called a Seashore Conservation Area, stretches a total of twenty-three miles and is under the jurisdiction of the ranger in charge of Twin Harbors State Park.

Float 20 Viewing & Fishing Pier

The public fishing pier on Float 20 can be reached from the parking lot near the Fisherman's Monument at the end of Neddie Rose Drive. A ramp leads to the

A favorite walk is out to the fishing pier which crosses by bridge to the wooden structure reaching out into the Harbor and gives an unparalleled view of Westport, Grays Harbor and the Olympic Mountains.

mooring docks. The walkway continues over a bridge to the long pier which extends into the Harbor, making it a great place to fish, to bird watch or to absorb the scenery.

Vista Viewing

A Viewing Tower at the end of Westhaven Drive is worth the climb to the top. Built by the Port of Grays Harbor in the late 1980s, the fifty-foot-tall structure affords a commanding view of Grays Harbor, Ocean Shores, both the North and South Jetties, and of course, the mighty Pacific.

At the foot of Neddie Rose Drive, there is a second opportunity to view Grays Harbor. A viewing platform perched atop the revetment rocks affords a sweeping view of the Ports of Aberdeen and Hoquiam, the Olympic Mountains, Ocean Shores and

At the corner of Westhaven and Neddie Rose Drives behind the revetment wall is a 50′ tall viewing tower which overlooks the mouth of Grays Harbor. Boat and ship traffic are almost constant.

the North Jetty across Grays Harbor, and the mighty Pacific beyond the Grays Harbor bar.

Veterans Memorial Park at the Isle of Flags

The Isle of Flags Park along South Montesano Street on City of Westport watershed property was dedicated in April 1986. Featured are flags from states of the Union and provinces of Canada. They fly from May to September from poles imbedded in blocks, with plaques inscribed with their geographic names and the names of individuals who financially sponsored them. Tiles with names of donors to the over-all project were laid between the two flag standards.

The City of Westport granted permission in 1994 to install in the Isle of Flags Park an All Veterans Memorial Wall. The wall is dedicated to any veteran of United States Military Forces, local or otherwise, who has served his or her country honor-

The Isle of Flags Park was dedicated in 1986. Flags of states and provinces of Canada fly during the summer months.

The All Veterans Memorial Wall was added to the Isle of Flags in 1996 and the City renamed the park Veterans Memorial Park at the Isle of Flags.

ably. Individual names are inscribed along with rank, year of birth and death, if applicable, or space to add the date when appropriate.

This project was made possible by $1,000 donations each from the estate of Father William G. Quick, The Ladies Auxiliary to General James H. Doolittle South Beach VFW Post No. 3057, the family of Robert M. Rogers, Lempi K. Lillegaard and Barbara M. Aue.

Inscriptions and future wall sections are financed by the subscribers. In 1996, the Westport City Council renamed the park Veterans Memorial Park At The Isle of Flags.

Seafood Festivals Bring City Park

Also notable was the 1914 purchase of a seven acre site for a city park by a group of Westport women. Adept in seafood cooking, they were able to raise the necessary money by holding community dinners. The first Seafood Festival was held that year. Since the end of World War II it has been an annual tradition. Many times the women of Westport have baked salmon, made clam chowder and served cracked crab for money-making projects. These ladies worked diligently to produce a park with water piped to camp sites and a shelter from the weather under an outdoor roofed kitchen. When paid for, the park was turned over to the city.

Recently, the day-use-only Westport City Park has been renovated. On the grounds are a large parking lot, a restroom, a covered picnic area, children's play-

A picnic of local people may have been held in the City Park, which was donated to the community by several ladies of early Westport.

ground, and a ball field. Trails wander through tree-covered dunes. The park was rededicated in memory of Harriet Nyhus Dorland on September 21, 1996.

Service & Social Organizations

Veterans of Foreign Wars

On August 9, 1941, a charter was granted by the Veterans of Foreign Wars of the United States for the establishment of South Beach VFW Post No. 3057. After the end of World War II, membership grew enough so that the old building in which they met was unsatisfactory. It was time to acquire property and build their own meeting hall. In 1948 the group purchased two lots located on East Pacific Avenue, one block east of Montesano Street, at a price of $231.81 from Henry Hinton. Westport City council

The Tablet was given by the Robert Gray Chapter of the Daughters of the American Revolution in 1929 and sits in City Park near the location where Fort Chehalis was built in 1860. Thor Lauritzen photo.

The City Park now has a playfield for children as well as a covered picnic area, parking lot and ballfield. Thor Lauritzen photo.

approved plans designed by Robert Smythe for a building estimated to cost $26,000. In order to pay for the project, five percent bonds were sold.

Ground was broken and construction work was undertaken, mostly by volunteer labor. The Ladies Auxiliary, consisting of VFW members, held many fund-raising events such as dinners and raffles to help cover the cost of materials. When the larger comfortable building was finished, it was dedicated on September 29, 1956. Twelve years later, the bonds were paid off. A huge celebration included the burning of the mortgage in a barbecue grill in the center of the dance floor in the Post building.

Due to the generosity of Dutch John Carstenson, a youth center was erected in the late 1960s. Located directly behind the Post Home, the building houses the VFW Auxiliary meetings, youth activities and community functions, such as meeting and receptions.

In August of 1974, the Altar Society of St. Paul Catholic Church sponsored a dinner for Medal of Honor recipients, fourteen of whom attended. Included among the dignitaries was Robert Bush, who at that time owned Bayview Lumber in Westport, and General James H. Doolittle. At the dinner it was discovered that the much-decorated General was not a VFW member. He was invited to join the local Post and graciously accepted. Doolittle made trips to Westport, becoming acquainted with and developing strong ties with Father Quick at St. Paul Church. Quick was a veteran of World War I. The two men went on fishing trips together each fall.

After the death of General Doolittle in 1994, the national headquarters of the VFW gave permission for the Westport Post to be renamed General James H. Doolittle South Beach Veterans of Foreign Wars Post No. 3057. The ceremony was attended by Mr. and Mrs. John Doolittle, son and daughter-in-law of the General, as well as Bush and several other Medal of Honor winners.

The VFW Ladies Auxiliary at Westport has received many awards for their work in the community. This involves not only help for families of veterans but also in other areas, such as coordinating children's activities, contributing to the local library and addressing health issues. They continue to hold fund-raising events to cover expenses incurred in their volunteer work. The local Auxiliary also supports the VFW National Home in Eaton Rapids, Michigan, for the benefit of widows and orphans of veterans.

American Legion

The Westport American Legion Post No. 140 was chartered on May 23, 1978, with thirty-two members. Auxiliary to Post No. 140, with fourteen members, was given its charter two years later.

This group does not have a building of its own but met in the John Carstenson Youth Center of the V.F.W. Post No. 3057 until 1982. Then they met in the Westport Lions' Hall for ten years. Since 1992, they again gather in the V.F.W. Youth Center. The combined group of seventy-nine members meets every fourth Tuesday for a business meeting and potluck supper.

Not having a meeting place of their own does in no way hinder the group from participating in volunteer services. Along with the V.F.W., they annually form the Color Guard and Marching Unit at four area parades, or whenever needed, such as Memorial Day Services. Donations are given to American Lake Hospital for Veterans, Western State Hospital and the the United States Veterans Homes in Retsil and in Orting. The United Services Organization (U.S.O.) Lounges at McChord Field and at SeaTac Airport are also recipients of gifts from Post No. 140.

Money for these and other projects is raised by a raffle held each year, and through the well-known annual poppy program. The Legionnaires have quietly continued to do what they can to give assistance to veterans and their families.

Clubs For Fun and Service To Others

Those who live in the South Beach area can join organizations such as the Lions, Moose, and Kiwanis Clubs, the Kinnikinnick Garden Club, AARP, the American Association of University Women, the Children's Hospital Auxiliary, and can participate in various senior citizens' activities. Self-help groups in the area also meet regularly.

In Conclusion

It is hard for us to imagine the wild and untamed country of Chehalis Point founded by the Speakes, the Petersons and the Luarks, as it would have been for any of those families to see the great changes that have taken place since their arrival. We can only admire the indomitable spirit of these early people who did what they could to tame the land and make it habitable for us to enjoy the opportunity of living comfortably in beautiful surroundings.

Appendix A

Westport Mayors

Mayor	Term Start
Lloyd Cook	1914
William Ingram	1915
Gustaf Nielson	1921
Fred M. Smith	1924
Eberhard Nyhus	1925
George W. Elliott	1928
William Ingram	1930
George W. Elliott	1931
Gustav Nielson	1932
McAdam	1934
William S. Tuthill	1934 (finished term)
C.M. Richardson	1935
E.W. Musgrave	1938
I.A. McDonald	1940
M.B. Mosher	1946
C.L. Wilson	1950
Bjarne Nilsen	1952
Byron Cramer	1964
Bjarne Nilsen	1968
Ralph Boohm	1969
William Wade	1973
Orville Engle	1980
Harold Hardy	1981
Robert Hepsoe	1990 (finished term)
Douglas Merino	1992
Drury Wood, Jr.	1996
Berkley Barker	1998
Michael Bruce	2004

Appendix B

Westport Postmasters

Name	Year Started
Thomas J. Carter	1860
Francis M. Stocking	1863
Patterson Luark	1864
Dudley S. B. Henry	1869
Mary A. Bergman	1870
Glenn Peterson	1870
Alexander Laidlaw	1887
Charles Yana	1890
Clara Scammon	1892
Robert Ogburn	1893
Thomas F. Thompson	1897
Ed. A. Bacon	1901
Frederick L. Rogers	1902
George N. Scammon	1911
Wm. R. Dibkey	1915
George W. Elliott	1915
Eberhard Nyhus	1920
Frank Wilkins	1923
Norman Wilkins	1924
Eberhard Nyhus	1933
Bonnie M. Wade (Name changed to Bonnie Miller)	1957
Harriet Nyhus Dorland	1973
Margaret Pierce	1985
Enola (Jinx) Stedman	1989
Anne Gabriel	1998

Appendix C

U.S. Lifesaving Station Keepers and Coast Guard Station Grays Harbor Commanding Officers Charles Jacobsen served as Grays Harbor Lifesaving Station Keeper from 1897 to 1917, the last two years as Grays Harbor Commanding Officer when the U.S. Lifesaving Service became a part of the U.S. Coast Guard.

COMMANDING OFFICER	START DATE
Roy Jacobsen	1920
Oscar C. Hawthorne	1920
Hilman Persson	1922
Leslie V. Barnett	1938

The U.S. Lifesaving Service joined the U.S. Coast Guard in 1939. During World War II, Van Hine and M.G. Alvey served as Commanding Officers.

W.G. Kincaide	1946
J.H. Miller	1948
E.S. Klock	1949
J.J. Hardy	1951
R.E. Miller	1951
T.B. Barnett	1952
R.W. Dowell	1955
D. Dixon	1955
F. Gold	1957
Lindquist	1958
W. Hake	1961
C. Lippincott	1964
Yarrington	1965
J.B. Alexander	1968
G.M. Vanderhoof	1971
W. Keith Herrell	1973
Chidester	1976
S.H. Smith	1979
J. Duncan	1982
S. Gordon	1985
Pat Trapp	1988
D.J. Booth	1991
Randy Lewis	1994
Walt Pedersen	1998
Michael Hoag	2000
Darrin Wallace	2003
J. Oglesby	2006
Jerry Farmer	2009
Gary Clark	2012

BIBLIOGRAPHY

Anderson, Bern, *The Life and Voyages of Captain George Vancouver, Surveyor of the Sea.* University of Washington Press, 1960.

Boit, John, *A New Log of the Columbia.* Massachusetts Historical Society, 1921.

Flynn, Thomas, *Westports of the Western World.* Westport, Ireland, 1961.

Gibbs, Jim, *Lighthouses of the Pacific.* Schiffer Press, 1986.

Hogan, Kathy, *Cohassett Beach Chronicles.* Oregon State University Press, 1995.

Janke, W. F., *Faith and Sweat.* Snohomish Publishing Co., 1977.

Luark, Patterson, *Journals 1852-68.* Washington State Library

McDonald, Lucile, *Coast Country.* Ilwaco Heritage Foundation, 1989.

Swan, James G., *Northwest Coast or Three Years Residence in Washington Territory. Harper Bros., 1857.*

Van Syckle, Edwin, *The River Pioneers.* Pioneer Press, 1982.

Van Syckle, Edwin, *They Tried to Cut It All.* Pacific Press. 1980.

The War of the Rebellion: *A Compilation of the Official Records of the Union and Confederate Armies.* Washington, Government Printing Office, 1897.

Washington - *A Guide to the Evergreen State.* Washington State Historical Society, W. P. A. Project, 1941.

Washington State Parks and Recreation Commission, *A History of Washington State Parks, 1913-1988,* Cherish the Treasure.

Williams, Herb, *Twin Harbor Tales.* 1967.

Work, John, *Journal of John Work, November and December 1824.* Washington Historical Quarterly 3, 1912.

INDEX

Photo by Thor Lauritzen

About the Author

Seattle native, Ruth L. McCausland, retired to Southwest Washington with her husband, Bob, a newspaper cartoonist, twenty years ago. An avid gardener and bird watcher, Ruth loves the outdoors along coastal Washington.

Since moving to the Tokeland area, the couple have been involved in historical projects, writings and artwork. They have two sons and two granddaughters.